DOES THE BIBLE REALLY SAY THAT?

DOES THE BIBLE REALLY SAY THAT?

EVERETT LEADINGHAM, EDITOR

Though this book is designed for group study, it is also intended for personal enjoyment and spiritual growth. A leader's guide is available from your local bookstore, publisher, or WordAction supplier.

Beacon Hill Press of Kansas City
Kansas City, Missouri

TABLE OF CONTENTS

PREFACE

What distinguishes the Christian believer from everyone else on the planet is the life-changing influence of Jesus Christ. What a person thinks of Him makes all the difference. Unfortunately, the world wouldn't bother to crucify the Jesus that many people today imagine Him to be. They have re-created Him in their own minds, giving Him a more acceptable *persona*—a mild-mannered, inoffensive figure who helps people to feel good about themselves. However, this is not the Jesus we meet in the Gospels. Jesus did not limit His teachings to things that were pleasant to hear. When Jesus walked the roads of ancient Israel, some loved Him for the redemptive change He had worked in them, and others hated Him because of things that He had said. And we still have those who are offended by Him today.

The Good News is that Christ Jesus comes into our lives to help us become the very best Christians we can be. Jesus makes it part of His agenda to raise questions about our questionable notions. He challenges our misconceptions. He identifies our mistaken priorities. And when He speaks, He calls us to think and to respond. That is why some of our Lord's teachings are called "hard." Because He loves us, He says the things that we need to hear, even when it may be painful.

The phrase, "hard teaching," is used to describe Jesus' words in the Bible one time:

> "Jesus said to them, 'I tell you the truth, unless you eat the flesh of the Son of Man and drink his blood, you have no life in you. Whoever eats my flesh and drinks my blood has eternal life, and I will raise him up at the last day. For my flesh is real food and my blood is real drink. Whoever eats my flesh and drinks my blood remains in me, and I in him. Just as the living Father sent me and I live because of the Father, so the one who feeds

on me will live because of me. This is the bread that came down from heaven. Your forefathers ate manna and died, but he who feeds on this bread will live forever.' He said this while teaching in the synagogue in Capernaum.

"On hearing it, many of his disciples said, 'This is a hard teaching. Who can accept it?'" (John 6:53-60).

A saying that is "hard" can have two meanings, either "hard to understand" or "hard to accept." Teachings that are "hard to accept" are those that challenge superficial discipleship with a call to a costly way of life. Teachings that are "hard to understand" are difficult to fit into what else we know about the Bible, or they reflect a historical situation that is enough different from our own to impede our understanding.

In the chapters that follow, we will be looking at hard teachings that fall into both categories. The sayings that are hard to understand can usually be clarified by adding some information about the historical background, the customs of the time, or the meaning of the words. However, when it comes to the sayings that are hard because people don't like what they say, no amount of clarification will help. In these instances, we can only give assurance that the Word means exactly what it says. Our aim with all these hard teachings is to arrive at the truth which sets us free.

THE DIFFICULT WORDS:

Everyone who speaks a word against the Son of Man will be forgiven, but anyone who blasphemes against the Holy Spirit will not be forgiven (Luke 12:10).

BACKGROUND SCRIPTURE: Luke 12:1-12

TRUTH TO REMEMBER:

While we believe that no one lies outside of the grace of God's redeeming power, there may be a point where we place ourselves outside of God's sphere of saving influence by denying or turning our back on Him.

GUIDANCE ALONG OUR JOURNEY:

Jesus warned His disciples to "beware" of the "hypocrisy" of the Pharisees. No one reading the Gospels can escape this constant message of our Lord: Beware of hypocrisy! It's a bit like hypertension—a silent, slow, deadly killer. Nothing seemed more serious to our Lord. Though He is sometimes portrayed as gently nonjudgmental and forever tolerant, in fact, Jesus had strong convictions and spoke words of condemnation. Some things cannot be tolerated! And nothing else, apparently, more seriously jeopardizes our relationship with the Father than hypocrisy. Truth denied long enough, like an unsharpened axe, loses its edge. Sadly enough, some of the Pharisees deceived themselves. They lied so well they believed their own lie! Such self-deceit, Jesus warned, leads to hard hearts. This is the essence of what Jesus calls "The sin against the Holy Spirit" (Luke 12:10b).

This chapter focuses on this hard saying of Jesus about "the unforgivable sin" (12:10). This subject has been often misrepresented and greatly misunderstood. We need this study for several reasons: (1) Jesus' warning needs to be heard today. He understands our natural tendency toward self-deception and can help us to remain sensitive to God. (2) We need to understand that it is unpardonable to become hardened and hostile to what is unmistakably divine. (3) This session will also challenge each of us to a deeper walk with God.

Chapter 1

THE SIN AGAINST THE HOLY SPIRIT

A GROUP OF PHARISEES has just had Jesus' words for lunch—literally. He gave them more to chew on than they wanted. He spoke to them so plainly that one of them commented, "Teacher, when you say these things, you insult us also" (Luke 11:45). Yet, Jesus went right on pronouncing His distress with them about the hardness of their hearts.

When Jesus left them, these Pharisees plotted among themselves against Him. And even though a crowd numbering in the thousands had gathered to hear Him speak, Jesus began by ministering to His disciples regarding what He had just experienced. "Be on your guard against the yeast of the Pharisees which is hypocrisy" (Luke 12:1*b*).

This encounter with the Pharisees sets the tone for all that Jesus has to say in Luke 12:1-12.

The Truth Will Come to Light

Jesus was troubled by the influence of the Pharisees, and yet the basic theology they espoused was closer to Jesus' own teachings than any other sect of that time.

- The Pharisees represented a longing for a righteous Israel.
- They promoted the hope of a coming Messianic Kingdom.
- It was supposed to be the goal of every Pharisee to bring all of life into subjection to the law.

Our Lord's complaint about the Pharisees was that they didn't live up to what they believed. Jesus called them "hypocrites." The word means "acting the part." They gave the appearance of religious devotion, but it was a disguise. Although they were spiritually impoverished, they appointed themselves as the spiritual guides for the people of God. Jesus called them "blind guides" (Matthew 15:14).

Sadly enough, they apparently deceived themselves. They lied so well they believed their own lie! We know this is possible, for the followers of Lenin persuaded themselves they should enslave people in order to ultimately free them. In the dramatic "purges" of the 1930s, prominent Bolsheviks confessed to crimes they knew they had not committed, all in support of the "cause." Similarly in Jesus' day, some Pharisees lived a lie so long they forgot it was a lie. Step-by-step, though proudly claiming to be Abraham's heirs, they forgot that to be blessed like Abraham, they must be holy like Abraham; that outward ceremonies avail nothing without inward purity, that their thoughts and motives must be heavenly.

Part of the sham of hypocrisy is the lie that "no one will ever know." Jesus declares that the play-actors must eventually face up to reality. The truth will be known. The things that have been hidden will be brought into the light for all to see.

No one can hide from God, and why would anyone want to? One of the defining realities for the person who walks with God has to do with what God knows. For the person who does not know God, the fact that nothing is hidden from Him is a frightening truth. For the person who walks with God, there is comfort and security in the realization that God knows about everything.

We Are the Objects of God's Care

In the space of four verses (Luke 12:4-7), Jesus speaks four times of fear, and the references are in striking contrast.

● "Do not be afraid . . ." (v. 4).

- "I will tell you whom you should fear: Fear him . . ." (v. 5).
- "I tell you, fear him . . ." (v. 5).
- "Don't be afraid" (v. 7).

We might expect Jesus to say, "Fear Satan," but He does not. In other scriptures we are told to "resist him" (James 4:7; 1 Peter 5:9), but we do not have to fear him.

Jesus tells us we are not to be afraid of what other people can do to us (v. 4). He points out that the worst other people can do is to kill us. And that is supposed to comfort us? Yes, it is. Over the centuries, in times of persecution, believers have been willing to exchange their earthly lives for a greater treasure—life eternal. In order to appreciate this life as we should, we need to remember that life in Christ has eternity in it!

What we are to fear is God himself (v. 5). We are to fear Him because our eternal destinies are in His hands. However, because we know Him, and because we have learned that He is trustworthy, the fear of God that once caused us to tremble now fills us with a sense of reverence and awe. Verses 6 and 7 tell us why we don't have to be afraid—because God cares for us.

It is meaningful that right after we are told that God is to be feared (v. 5), we are reminded that God can be trusted (vv. 6-7).

God Is Ready to Forgive Every Sin

Jesus teaches very clearly in Luke 12:8-12 that anyone who blasphemes against the Holy Spirit will not be forgiven. Yet, this is not the only occasion when Jesus spoke about this unpardonable sin (see Matthew 12:31-32; Mark 3:28-30). In those instances, Jesus was addressing individuals who opposed Him, and He warned them about it for their own good. In the passage before us, Jesus is speaking words of encouragement chiefly to His disciples. In this setting, His words about the unpardonable sin are spoken to assure them that anyone who blasphemes the Holy Spirit will have to face the consequences. Verses 11 and 12 imply that it was His purpose to prepare the disciples for times that were coming when His enemies would try to intimidate them. He was arming them with the truth that those whose hearts were hopelessly hardened to the voice of the Holy Spirit were already facing the penalty of God's judgment.

We need to ask what it is about "blasphemy against the Holy Spirit" that makes it unforgivable. Awful though "deadly sins," such as pride, envy, anger, lust, and sloth, may be, they do not qualify as "unforgivable." Horrendous acts, such as brutal serial murders, do not necessarily insulate one from the Holy Spirit's convicting power. Even angry outbursts, such as atheists blaming God for the ills of the world, may be revoked through repentance and worship of the living Lord.

Sin is "unforgivable" when hardness of heart results from habitual dishonesty and persistent denial—the refusal to face and rightly deal with the truth.

Pilate's "What is truth?" question, posed to justify his refusal to deal with it, typifies the attitude which becomes resistance to God. Pharisaical strategies, substituting "religious" standards which please people rather than being true to God's divinely revealed standards, slowly separate a person from the convicting voice of the Holy Spirit. Walking away from the Light of the World, preferring to live in sin's darkness, unwilling to even think about seeking the Truth, ultimately leaves a person stranded so deep in the cave that no light can penetrate.

Blasphemy against the Holy Spirit is not a specific sin, but a condition which limits what God can do in the life of the unrepentant, unconcerned individual.

F. F. Bruce once said that there are few more distressing conditions calling for treatment by caretakers of souls than that of people who believe they have committed the unpardonable sin. A classic example of what Bruce meant is the English poet, William Cowper (1731-1800) [pronounced "Cooper"]. Cowper was convinced throughout life that he had committed the unpardonable sin.

When he was 21, he entered the legal profession. Later, he was nominated to be a clerk in the House of Lords. However, under the strain of preparing for the examination, he had a mental breakdown. Cowper tried to kill himself.

In 1763, he was confined in St. Alban's asylum for 18 months, convinced that God was punishing him. During his confinement, while he was being visited by his brother, William Cowper gained his senses long enough to experience conversion and the certainty of forgiveness from sin. Unfortunately, that was not the end of his struggles. He suffered from extended periods of melancholy and despondency until his death in 1800, still convinced that he had committed the unpardonable sin.

However, in spite of his struggles, he is considered the greatest poet of his generation. And he remains one of the most-quoted of all the English poets, with lines, such as "Variety's the very spice of life." He wrote many well-loved hymns, including "There Is a Fountain," "O for a Closer Walk with God," and "God Moves in a Mysterious Way." He became a close friend of John Newton. Together they conducted prayer meetings, visited the sick, and assisted the poor. They collaborated on a collection of hymns called "The Olney Hymns," which was a landmark in Christian hymnody. John Newton wrote 281 of the hymns, and William Cowper wrote 67.

Cowper battled his religious doubts and fears to the end of his life. He felt that God had damned him "below Judas Iscariot." He had persistent dreams about God's vengeance on him. William Cowper is representative of many who have suffered unnecessarily because they have misunderstood Jesus' teaching about the unpardonable sin.

If only he could have heard Adam Clarke make this point: "The unpardonable sin, as some term it, is neither less nor more than ascribing the miracles Christ wrought, by the power of God, to the spirit of the devil . . . No man who believes the Divine mission of Jesus Christ, ever can commit this sin."*

---

*Adam Clarke, *The New Testament of our Lord and Saviour Jesus Christ* (New York: Abingdon Press, n.d.), 5:138.

Sincere believers need not worry that they have committed the unpardonable sin. It's the ones who don't care if they have who likely will do it.

THE DIFFICULT WORDS:

If anyone comes to me and does not hate his father and mother, his wife and children, his brothers and sisters—yes, even his own life—he cannot be my disciple (Luke 14:26).

BACKGROUND SCRIPTURE: Luke 14:25-35

TRUTH TO REMEMBER:

Believers are called to a level of devotion to Jesus Christ so all-encompassing that all other allegiances pale by comparison.

GUIDANCE ALONG OUR JOURNEY:

This is the second chapter on verses in the New Testament that are hard to understand. The previous chapter's hard saying dealt with Jesus' words about "the sin against the Holy Spirit," also known as "the unpardonable sin." We found that no one is outside of God's love, and the only one who cannot be forgiven is the one who does not want to be forgiven.

In the Scripture focus for this chapter, our Lord's teaching about hating one's family—and one's own life—is difficult in more than one way: It was very hard for people to understand what Jesus meant. And when they did grasp the meaning of Jesus' words, it was a truth that was not easy for them to accept. This is equally true for us.

It is not a coincidence that Luke was led to tell about the large crowds that were following Jesus (14:25). This kind of following would have been a great delight to almost anyone else. However, Jesus was concerned about their reasons for following Him. He could not be satisfied for His people to have shallow, superficial motives. For those who would follow Him, Jesus wanted to be sure that they understood the great importance of God's clear call! Everything else must come in no better than second place—not even those who are dearest to us. Only God could demand the devotion that Jesus called His followers to demonstrate (see Deuteronomy 6:4-5).

Chapter 2

HATING ONE'S FAMILY

RABBI TARFON'S MOTHER tore her sandal walking in her courtyard on the Sabbath. Because she was devoted to the Law, she could not repair the damage on the Holy Day. Walking with at least one foot bare seemed her only option. Out of respect for his mother, Tarfon placed his hands under the soles of her feet so she could walk on his hands until she reached the couch.

Later when the rabbi was sick, the sages came to visit him. His mother said, "Pray for my son Tarfon, for he treats me with too much honor."

"In what way?" they asked her.

When she told the story of the split sandal, they said, "Even if he did what you say—did so a thousand thousand times—he still has not come halfway to showing the full honor that the Torah says a son owes a parent."[1]

A Long-Standing Tradition

This story of a Jewish family in New Testament times illustrates a central truth in Judaism. The devout were taught that only one person dare be given more respect and honor than their parents—God himself.

Can you picture Jesus about to die on the Cross? As a good Jewish son, He looked down at His mother and said to her, "'Dear woman [a term of endearment], here is your son,' and to [John] the disciple, 'Here is your mother.' From that time on, this disciple took her into his home" (John 19:26-27). Jesus' care for His mother at the time of His own death was in keeping with the very best of Jewish tradition.

The scene from Golgotha reminds us of David running for his life from a furious and dangerous King Saul. Finding a temporary home in Mizpah, he asked the king of Moab what any good Hebrew man would ask, "Would you let my father and mother come and stay with you until I learn what God will do for me?" (1 Samuel 22:3). The king honored his request. From before David until long after Jesus was here on earth, children's duty to their parents has been a primary concern of Judaism.

In fact, Jesus scolded some religious leaders of His day for their money-grabbing attitudes that allowed them to "legally" ignore their duty to their parents. His respect for the ancient teaching to honor fathers and mothers brought Him into conflict with those teachers of the Law who declared a gift Corban (see Mark 7:9-13). "Corban" is a Hebrew term meaning "set apart for God." By New Testament times if a person declared some of his assets Corban, he would not have to give that money to support his parents in their old age. Instead, he could use it for investment and speculation until he died, then it would be given to the Temple in his honor and memory.

In light of such long-standing tradition, how then could Jesus say, "If anyone comes to me and does not hate his father and mother, his wife and children, his brothers and sisters— yes, even his own life—he cannot be my disciple" (Luke 14:26)? In order to understand this difficult teaching, we will need to reconsider what Jesus was saying.

A New Definition

There are only a few watershed events in any nation's history. These defining moments determine the character and destiny of a country and its people. For example, few, if any, United States presidents have captured the moment and turned history on its hinges as Abraham Lincoln did on January 1, 1863 when he signed the Emancipation Proclamation. Though it freed very few slaves at the time, the Proclamation defined the future of freedom from slavery in the United States forever.

One of those defining moments for the Hebrews came when Moses, standing near the Jordan River, called the people together and talked to them about the promises that had been made at Sinai. He reminded them that the Sinai covenant was not simply a historical document between their fathers and God, a relationship of value only to their ancestors. It was, in fact, a living reality which, even at that moment, controlled their lives and their destiny (see Deuteronomy 5:1-3). Then, having recounted the "word of the Lord" (which we know as the Ten Commandments) that would forever guide them, Moses turned to the future. A future across the river that would not include him but must include that covenant-making God in order for them to be successful in building both personal character and their nation.

The climactic moment came when Moses said, "Hear, O Israel: The LORD our God, the LORD is one" (Deuteronomy 6:4). The God who delivered them from Egypt. The God of salvation-history. This God is one God, not many gods. It was an unabashed, unashamed, undiluted proclamation that there is only one God, not a family of gods. We cannot understand the Bible without accepting the central place of this theological cornerstone: God is one.

When Jesus was asked which of the commandments was the greatest, He replied, "The most important one . . . is this: 'Hear, O Israel, the Lord our God, the Lord is one" (Mark 12:29). Not a handful of gods. Not a collection of gods. "The Lord is one." Then Jesus added from the ancient Word, "Love the Lord your God with all your heart and with all your soul and with all your mind and with all your strength" (v. 30).

Only One Worthy

We began this chapter with a story from the life of Rabbi Tarfon. We noted that his experience with his mother illustrates a central truth in Judaism. The devout were taught that they dared to give only one person more respect and honor than their parents—God himself.

In a subtle way that the ancients would have understood more easily than we, Jesus affirmed His deity when He spoke about family loyalties. The Greek word Luke uses in this passage that is translated "hate" is a strong word meaning "despise" or "abhor." However in a companion passage, Matthew records Jesus saying, "Anyone who *loves* his father or mother more than me is not worthy of me; anyone who *loves* his son or daughter more than me is not worthy of me" (10:37, emphasis added).

Most commentators on this passage of scripture see Jesus' saying to "hate" one's family as a vivid hyperbole meant to call the listeners' (and readers') attention to His words. Jesus used hyperboles (extravagant exaggerations) in other instances —like the time he talked about "beams" and "splinters" in eyes and when he talked about "plucking one's eye out" or "cutting one's hand off"—to make a point with such dramatic impact that people would listen.

Whether the verb is "to hate," "to ignore," or "to love more than," the message is the same. Jesus calls for greater loyalty to Him than that given to even the most beloved on earth.

Since the Torah taught that God is the only one worthy of more honor and respect than one's parents, it follows that when Jesus calls for that greater devotion, He is declaring that He is God himself. For the Jews and for us, these words redefine who Jesus is. Yet, there is more. These words call for . . .

A New Calculation of the Cost

Luke repeats the obvious, "Large crowds were traveling with Jesus" (14:25). And no wonder. A radio commentator came to our town the other day, a man who has become famous for making sarcastic remarks about the president of the

United States. The auditorium couldn't hold the number of people who wanted to hear their national leader abused. That's one reason the crowds followed Jesus. You just never knew when He would launch an attack on some public personality for private misdeeds.

Then there were the miracles. Blind men seeing. Lame walking. Demons scattered into a herd of pigs. Now that's interesting! What wonderful stories to tell around the campfire at night. And perhaps, just maybe, this Jesus might be the Messiah the prophets talked about, the One some were now saying would lead a revolution against Rome. You never knew what adventure lay around the corner. So the crowds gathered. They didn't want to miss the action.

Jesus needed the crowds, but not because He was an entertainer. Talking to the wind or shouting into the whirlwind will not win many converts to a new idea. Jesus needed an audience to hear His message of spiritual freedom, love, and peace. Mark tells us that, for a while, "The large crowd listened to him with delight" (12:37).

Then, there came a moment when things changed. Each of the Gospels records what happened as the crowd gradually understood the radical nature of Christ's message. John tells us, in relation to another event, that so many people deserted Jesus the Lord questioned whether the apostles wanted to leave also (6:6-67).

Jesus is calling us to a level of devotion so all-encompassing that all other allegiances look like hate by comparison.

By the time he was 30 years of age, Albert Schweitzer (1875-1965) was known as a preacher, educator, author, musician, and philosopher. He had received three doctoral degrees. He was principal of a theological college. He was a noted organist, a leading interpreter of the works of Bach.

In spite of his achievements, Albert Schweitzer struggled over these words of Jesus: "Whosoever will save his life shall lose it; but whosoever shall lose his life for my sake and the gospel's, the same shall save it" (Mark 8:35, KJV). Then in the fall of 1904, he read that the Paris Missionary Society needed workers in Africa. The article concluded, "Men and women who can reply simply to the Master's call, 'Lord, I am coming,' those are the people whom the Church needs." Schweitzer later testified, "My search was over." He would dedicate the rest of his life to the service of humanity.

On October 13, 1905, Schweitzer mailed letters from Paris, telling his family and closest friends about his plans to go to Africa as a missionary doctor. In the months that followed, he was tormented by both relatives and friends, who tried to convince him of his "folly." His suitability was even questioned by officers of the Paris Missionary Society.

For Albert Schweitzer to obey his call, his devotion to God had to become so complete that his love for those who were dearest to him was like hatred by comparison. All who walk with Him are called to that same level of devotion.

A New Family

On one hand, Jesus is calling us to a level of devotion so all-encompassing that all other allegiances look like hate by comparison. That's more than most of us can handle in a single dose, but it's not the full message of this passage.

Jesus calls His followers to become members of a new family. "A Christian's only relatives are the saints," said one of the early martyrs.[2] Jesus taught this long before that believer died for his faith.

One of the tragedies of Jesus' walk through life is that His family did not walk with Him. John comments, "Even his own brothers did not believe in him" (7:5). Mark records that when Jesus' family heard what He was doing and how the crowds reacted to Him, "They went to take charge of him, for they said, 'He is out of his mind'" (3:21). However, Jesus was not ready to be forced into seclusion as families used to hide the "funny" uncle away from public view. He asked, "'Who are my mother and my brothers?' Then he looked at those seated in a circle around him and said, 'Here are my mother and my brothers! Whoever does God's will is my brother and sister and mother'" (3:33-35).

Even in this day with the disintegration of many families, the majority of people are a part of a functioning family, one that provides love and security and to which they can return devotion and care. Sometimes in certain places in the world, a person's decision to follow Christ breaks the family apart and leaves the believer on the outside. At times, believers are banished, shunned by their loved ones. In the words quoted above, Jesus is saying that a new family is being created for all those who have been expelled from an earthly family because of their faith.

That's good news, but there's more.

Anyone who contemplates following Jesus must love Him much more than even their closest family members. This is not to say that their love for family must diminish; rather, it is to say that their love for Christ must increase and become supreme.

Our Lord declares that faith in Him develops a tie that binds people closer together than even sharing the same parents and grandparents. This new family is bonded together by believers' common love of Jesus and their devotion to His kingdom. Thus the call to follow Jesus is more than a call to be willing to say "good-bye" to life's best relationships, if that is the result of our confession of faith in Him. It is also an invitation to join a new family—the family of God. What an opportunity! What a privilege!

It is possible to be a follower of Jesus without being a disciple; to be a camp-follower without being a soldier of the king; to be a hanger-on in some great work without pulling one's weight. Once, someone was talking to a great scholar about a younger man. He said, "So and so tells me that he was one of your students." The teacher answered devastatingly, "He may have attended my lectures, but he was *not* one of my students."

It is one of the supreme handicaps of the Church that it has so many distant followers of Jesus and so few real disciples. What a responsibility we have to make sure that the Christian family lives up to its high calling in Christ.

Notes:

1. Hayim Nahman Bialik and Yehoshua Hana Riivnitsky, eds., *The Book of Legends*, translated by William G. Braude (New York: Shocken Books, 1992), 231.

2. William Barclay, *The Gospel of Matthew* (Philadelphia: The Westminster Press), 59.

THE DIFFICULT WORDS:

Do not suppose that I have come to bring peace to the earth. I did not come to bring peace, but a sword (Matthew 10:34).

BACKGROUND SCRIPTURE: Matthew 10:17-36

TRUTH TO REMEMBER:

The kingdom of God and all who pledge allegiance to it are automatically at odds with the kingdom of the world.

GUIDANCE ALONG OUR JOURNEY:

We are engaged in a conflict: The kingdom of this world is pitted against the kingdom of God. We know that God's kingdom will ultimately triumph. Yet in the meantime, believers are engaged in hand-to-hand combat with the forces of evil.

Our Lord has never tried to hide the truth about this kingdom conflict. In fact, He has always made it clear that anyone who followed Him would have to bear a cross (Mark 8:34). He even said that the cross would have to be carried daily (Luke 9:23). On one occasion, He told the crowds, "In this world you will have trouble." Yet, He told them this so He could also reassure them, "But take heart! I have overcome the world" (John 16:33).

In the focus for this chapter, Jesus is speaking once again about this kingdom conflict. This is another of the sayings of Christ that is hard to understand. It is difficult because it seems to be contrary to the mission of Christ. However, He is truthfully reminding believers that they will be confronted with opposition, that they will be at odds with this world.

Many of us have experienced hostility or rejection because of our faith in Christ. This chapter reminds all of us that there are occasions when the voices of this world speak out against the gospel and anyone who adheres to it. Still, the Christ who calls for our allegiance to Him also enables us to triumph by our faith in Him.

Chapter 3

NOT PEACE BUT A SWORD

THE ROMANS CALLED it *iter principis*, the "itinerary of the prince." The Greeks started the custom, but the Romans developed it into an effective imperial propaganda machine. Accompanied by his personal troops dressed in their sharpest uniforms, Caesar would tour the distant provinces. He rode from city to city in an elegant, horse-drawn vehicle or was carried on a litter, like an ancient Chinese emperor. When the procession approached a major city, the Roman ruler changed into his ceremonial battle armor and mounted a powerful white horse, entering the city as a victorious military leader. The local residents lined the streets, waving palm branches, the universal symbol of victory. If the people had been loyal to the throne, Caesar would confer special honors or privileges on the city and its residents.

The day after Jesus raised Lazarus from the dead, our Lord continued His *iter principis*, His journey toward His final destiny in Jerusalem. All four Gospels record the event we know as the Triumphal Entry, but John 12 gives us a special insight into what happened.

As the chief priests feared, the news of Lazarus swept through the city like wildfire. The crowd rushed to Bethany to see the once-dead man and, especially, the One who had defeated death, Jesus. The excited crowd cut palm branches and shouted, "Blessed is he who comes in the name of the Lord," quoting Psalm 118:26. Significantly, they added these words recorded only by John, "Blessed is the King of Israel!" (12:13).

John then says, "Jesus found a young donkey and sat upon it, as it is written, 'Do not be afraid, O Daughter of Zion; see, your king is coming, seated on a donkey's colt'" (vv. 14-15). Seeing that some in the crowd wanted to make Him their warrior-king, Jesus deliberately chose to ride the animal of peace —a donkey.

Familiar with the Roman *iter principis*, the crowd understood the symbolism. Yet, this is the One who earlier said, "Do not suppose that I have come to bring peace to the earth. I did not come to bring peace, but a sword" (Matthew 10:34).

A Look at the Tension

Matthew's Gospel was addressed primarily to Jewish believers in Christ. In fact, at the time he wrote his Gospel, there were still close connections between Christian believers and Jewish synagogues. Jewish believers participated in the life of the synagogue. In the early years following Christ's death, the message of Christ spread within synagogue fellowships. However, the time came when Christian believers were forced out of the synagogues. At the same time, the Church began reaching a predominantly Gentile audience. Paul's missionary strategy offers partial evidence of the transitions in location and membership. When he entered a new town, Paul first went to the local synagogue and preached Christ. He continued there, reasoning with Jews and explaining Scripture, until he was forced to leave. Then he helped to establish Jewish believers in the Christian faith while he proceeded to proclaim the Good News in the Gentile "public square."

Matthew's audience knew firsthand how divisive the gospel could be. The good news about Jesus was supposed to bring harmony and reconciliation, not only between individuals and God but also between people. However, the stark reality was that many Jewish Christians were driven away from their families because of their new faith. They knew what Jesus meant when He warned them about false accusations, beatings, betrayal, hatred, murder, and persecution. We know that many of them were handed over, arrested, flogged, and cast out.

It is ironic that division could be caused by the gospel of peace and love. Clearly, the gospel is about peace, love, mercy, forgiveness, and reconciliation. However, it also creates tension, as the world does not always respond with acceptance to its message. Their opposition creates division, sometimes leading to violence. Often, those who reject the gospel falsely accuse those who believe it. The tension in relationships is brought on by those who turn their backs on God's gift of mercy.

Let's look at the tension. Not the tension between a warrior-king and Jesus, but the conflict between what Jesus did to define who He was and what He and others said about His person and ministry.

Note the prophetic word: "For to us a child is born, to us a son is given, and the government will be on his shoulders. And he will be called Wonderful Counselor, Mighty God, Everlasting Father, Prince of Peace" (Isaiah 9:6). The kings of Isaiah's day governed poorly, were powerless in war, and unable to bring prosperity or peace. Isaiah looked forward to the One who would not be a failure, One who would fulfill all these promises. Generations later, that One born in Bethlehem was to be known as the Prince of Peace. And yet when that baby became a man, He said, "I did not come to bring peace, but a sword."

Hear the angelic announcement: One night long after Isaiah's time, the angels sang to a few shepherds on the hillside, "Glory to God in the highest, and on earth peace" (Luke 2:14). The baby they sang about would become a peaceable man who was often hounded by the forces of darkness. Yet, always loving, always in control, He would say to His disciples one day, "I did not come to bring peace, but a sword."

Listen to Jesus' promise: A few hours before His arrest in Gethsemane, Jesus said to His closest friends, "Peace I leave with you; my peace I give you. I do not give to you as the world gives. Do not let your hearts be troubled and do not be afraid" (John 14:27). Strangely, He was the same one who said, "I did not come to bring peace, but a sword."

Recall Christ's words after the Resurrection: "On the evening of that first day of the week [following His crucifixion], when the disciples were together, with the doors locked for fear of the Jews, Jesus came and stood among them and said, 'Peace be with you!'" (John 20:19). And yet earlier He had said to them, "I did not come to bring peace, but a sword."

A Look Beyond the Tension

One thing is certain: Jesus did not advocate conflict. He taught His followers to offer no resistance or retaliation when they were attacked or mistreated. In His Sermon on the Mount, He said, "Blessed are the peacemakers" (Matthew 5:9).

Still, some people have made a career by being heartless. One famous playwright said that critics "know the price of everything and the value of nothing."

Jesus didn't fit that definition. He knew value when He saw it. Matthew tells us that when Jesus "saw the crowds, he had compassion on them, because they were harassed and helpless, like sheep without a shepherd" (9:36). We know Jesus was compassionate so we've made this a "nice" little verse. That's because none of the English translations carry the almost animal-like fury of the original word translated "compassion."

We begin to catch the power of these words when we read the climax of a powerful story in Acts 1:18, "With the reward he got for his wickedness, Judas bought a field; there he fell headlong, his body burst open and all his intestines spilled out." The word translated "compassion" and the word "intestines" come from the same root in the Greek. We're more apt to say that when Jesus looked at the crowds, His "heart broke." Yet, the Greek says that when Jesus saw the crowd, He "felt it in His gut."

The phrase, "He felt it in His gut," may be a bit offensive to some, especially when it reports something Jesus felt. That's why the translations have domesticated it. But think about it for a moment. When you are frightened nearly out of your wits, where do you feel it? In the pit of your stomach, that's where. When you see something revolting, what's your reaction? You say it "turns my stomach," which is almost literally true. We prefer the word "visceral," a polite word for "in the guts." The Greeks called it the *splanchna*—the very depths of a person's being. *Splanchna* (pronounced SPLANK-nah) was their strongest word for compassion or pity.

So when we hear Jesus say, "I did not come to bring peace, but a sword," we must understand that His words did not come from a relaxed conversation around the campfire at the end of the day, but from the *splanchna*. This was no casual episode in our Master's life. He was as deeply moved as a person can ever be.

What did the disciples see when they looked at the crowds that pushed in on Jesus? In a word, trouble. Or at the very least, inconvenience and frustration. Note a couple examples. When a large crowd gathered in a remote place and stayed until past time for the evening meal, the disciples said, "Send the crowds away, so they can go to the villages and buy themselves some food" (Matthew 14:14). But Jesus, having had *splanchna* (the same word as in Matthew 9:36) enough to heal their sick, took a boy's lunch and fed 5,000 men, plus women and children.

One day when mothers crowded around Jesus, seeking His hand of blessing on their little children, "the disciples rebuked those who brought them" (Matthew 19:13). Likely the disciples thought Jesus was too busy for the unimportant ones. They were wrong!

What stirred Jesus to the depth—to His *splanchna?* He said that the crowd was "like sheep without a shepherd" (9:36). That's where we must begin to look, if we are to find meaning beyond the tension created by Jesus' words.

The Old Testament prophets paint the same picture. Holding in contempt the empty sources of guidance and help, Zechariah said, "The people wander like sheep oppressed for lack of a shepherd" (10:2).

Note that the prophet didn't say the people were leaderless. Rather, they were oppressed. Oppressed by their shepherd-leaders. That's the idea Jesus conveys here. The oppressors were the ones who should have been their spiritual guides and protectors, their supposed spiritual leaders—who appear often throughout the Scriptures as shepherds. Too often they were false shepherds. Zechariah delivers a devastating indictment of these unfaithful shepherds who lead the people into idol worship instead of the way of the Lord. Zechariah, speaking for the Lord, says, "My anger burns against the shepherds, and I will punish the leaders" (10:3). The power of divine anger and the urgency of the task lurks in the shadows as Jesus "saw the crowds, [and] had compassion on them, because they . . . were like sheep without a shepherd."

The Focus of the Tension

Quiet bystanders rarely cause conflict. Jesus asked the Lord of the harvest to send workers into the harvest field (Matthew 9:38). Immediately He began to answer His own prayer. He called the 12 disciples to Him and gave them the same authority He had over the devil and his demons. Then all of Satan's forces broke loose against Jesus and His disciples. The powers of darkness, alive and dangerously evil, were enfleshed in governors and kings, leaders of local councils, and synagogue rulers. All were arrayed against those who would take the gospel message of freedom from sin to the harassed and helpless crowd.

Jesus declared that the message would meet resistance. That resistance would come from many places, sometimes from one's own family. "Brother will betray brother to death, and a father his child; children will rebel against their parents and have them put to death" (10:21). The bold, aggressive witness of the disciples would be met with violence—a sword. Jesus calls His followers to be true to the end, but alerts them that their choice to follow Him will lead them on a dangerous road.

Three times in this passage, Jesus admonishes His disciples, "Do not be afraid" (vv. 26, 28, 31). It is no wonder He said this! This passage is not for the weak of heart. With all the talk of rejection, persecution, death, and betrayal, the natural response would be to be afraid.

One group of Christians who put into literal practice the words of Jesus, "I did not come to bring peace, but a sword," were the Crusaders of the Middle Ages. These warriors were intent on rescuing the Holy Land from the hands of the occupying Muslims. They were known for their ruthlessness and bloodshed, directed against anyone they perceived as an enemy of the Church. But Jesus counsels His disciples to opt for another perspective, a viewpoint that knows that no created thing or no created institution can make ultimate claims upon us.

We are told that more Christians were killed for their faith in the 20th century than ever before. Yet, most of us don't face the possibility of estrangement from our families because of our religious choices. Nor are we threatened with violence or death when we choose to witness for Jesus. Perhaps because faith carries no penalty and witnessing no danger, some have found it convenient to conclude that one religion is as good as another. That means that witnessing for their faith has no urgency. That stance also means they'll likely never understand what Jesus meant when He said, "I did not come to bring peace, but a sword."

Christ brings peace to the world, but not on the world's terms—the cessation of conflict that comes from compromise. His peace is the conquest of right over wrong, of righteousness over evil. He began His public career hovered over by the dove of peace and ended it hanging between heaven and earth on a cross of execution. Both the dove of peace and the violence of the Cross are symbols of His kingdom. The only real peace we can know in this world comes by submission to the authority of the warrior-king, the Prince of Peace. Then, and only then, His indwelling Spirit brings peace, a restored and happy relationship with the Lord. It is a peace that the world cannot give nor can it take away.

THE DIFFICULT WORDS:

Go, sell everything you have and give to the poor, and you will have treasure in heaven. Then come, follow me (Mark 10:21).

BACKGROUND SCRIPTURE: Mark 10:17-31

TRUTH TO REMEMBER:

The barrier all "would-be" disciples of Jesus face is an unreserved dedication to Him.

GUIDANCE ALONG OUR JOURNEY:

The Scripture focus for this chapter is Mark 10:17-31. This is another one of the hard sayings spoken by Jesus. The passage is commonly referred to as "The Rich Young Ruler" or "The Rich Young Man." This incident is considered so significant that it is included in all three of the synoptic Gospels (see also Matthew 19:16-30; Luke 18:18-30). Matthew tells us that he was young, and Luke informs us that he was a ruler. However, it is Mark who tells us that he "ran" to Jesus and "fell on his knees" before Him (Mark 10:17). It is also Mark who tells us that when Jesus looked at him, He loved him (v. 21).

The most significant fact about this encounter between Christ and the rich young man is that our Lord called him to join His circle of disciples and follow Him (v. 21). Yet, the young man who came running to Jesus with enthusiasm walked away in sadness. He considered the cost of following Christ too great to pay, because it would cost him everything. The truth of this passage is that all who follow Christ must give Him everything, holding nothing back. Later, with his usual "tact and charm," Peter reminded the Lord that all the disciples had left everything to follow Him (v. 28). Nevertheless, Jesus said they would receive far more than they would ever give.

Our Lord's call to the rich young man reminds us of believers who have left everything to follow Christ. Men like Frances of Assisi, who gave up the riches of his merchant father to walk with Christ in poverty. Women like Mother Teresa, who gave up her comfortable life in a wealthy home in order to minister to those who were left abandoned to die on the streets of Calcutta. Missionaries like Harmon Schmelzenbach, who left the comforts of his homeland to preach among the natives of Africa. Everyone who truly follows Christ will have as their model the One who "though he was rich, yet for [our] sakes he became poor, so that [we] through his poverty might become rich" (2 Corinthians 8:9).

Chapter 4

SELL EVERYTHING!

THE POOR MAKE us uncomfortable. Having successfully escaped to the suburbs where the homeless, hungry, and poverty-stricken are camouflaged if not completely hidden, we often avoid any place where the broken and bleeding edge of human sorrow can be seen.

The poor-by-choice are an even bigger problem for us. They challenge some of our basic assumptions about life—the importance of succeeding financially and what we gently call "middle-class values." That is, if purchasing a lot of unneeded things on an overburdened credit card and taking them home in an overpriced car to a heavily mortgaged home can be called a "value."

People have had difficulty with the poor-by-choice for a long time. In 1182, Francis was born Giovanni Francesco Bernadone, son of a wealthy Italian cloth merchant in Assisi. In his early 20s, disenchanted with materialism, he renounced his inherited wealth and gave his possessions to the poor. Then, he left home, dressed in a ragged cloak and the rope belt from a scarecrow. His father legally disinherited him; his church didn't know what to do with him. Though he did not aggressively seek converts to his simpler way of life, many people chose to follow his example. Soon a new order, the Franciscans, was approved by the pope.

However—and the story is too long to tell here—before many years had passed, the Franciscan order changed its nature completely, becoming an elaborate organization with expensive churches and schools.

To be poor-by-choice is not "normal."

The Jewish culture into which Jesus was born was not much different. They didn't know how to handle the poor-by-choice either. In fact, they had rules forbidding it. The rabbis of Jesus' day taught that you were not to give away more than 20 percent of your wealth, lest you become a burden on society. In a commentary on Deuteronomy 28:15-58, one rabbi wrote, "No portion in life is harder to bear than poverty, for he who is crushed by poverty is as one beset by all the afflictions in the world, indeed, as one stricken by the curses listed in Deuteronomy."[1]

Nor do we want to be poor-by-choice. That's what makes these words from Jesus as difficult today as they were when He first spoke them, "One thing you lack," Jesus said. "Go, sell everything you have and give to the poor, and you will have treasure in heaven. Then come, follow me" (Mark 10:21). On reflection, we'll see that these words talk to us about tough love and tough luck.

Tough Love

When you take a step back and look at it, this is an amazing story. Because wealth was considered a sign of God's favor, rabbis were expected to be financially secure. They didn't have to be wealthy but needed to be at least moderately well-to-do to have the respect of the community. But Jesus wasn't. He was a homeless, wandering preacher, with no dependable income. However, something about Him generated great respect. An important man came running after Jesus as He left town. It appears that the man was afraid of missing Him and, having stopped Jesus, knelt before Him.

What an astonishing event! Matthew, Mark, and Luke all identify the one who knelt as a very rich man. In addition, Matthew records that he was young (19:20); Luke adds that he was a ruler (18:18). So we call him "the rich young ruler." This man had everything: youth, riches, prestige, and power in the community—a combination most people in every generation would love to have. Yet with it all, he knelt before Jesus.

Jesus loved him even though he gave an incomplete answer to Jesus. This young man had tried his best to be good, to keep all the commandments since his childhood. However, "Jesus looked at him and loved him" (v. 21) and pressed on to the one thing the young man still needed.

The advantaged people in any community, those with power and money, may be honored but are not always loved. In fact, they are often viewed with a jealousy that questions both the way they obtained their money and spend it or the way they exercise their power. Yet, Jesus loved this young man who had everything people considered valuable. The word Mark uses here to describe Jesus' love is the great Christian word for love, *agape*, expressed most fully in Christ's sacrificial death on the Cross. It has no relation to erotic love and far exceeds the love of one friend for another.

Nor was Jesus an idle spectator. John tells us that Jesus "needed no one to testify about anyone; for he himself knew what was in everyone" (2:25, NRSV). We may safely conclude that Jesus knew that the young man kneeling before Him was an honest seeker after truth, a devout man who sincerely wanted to follow Him.

Yet, the man asked the wrong question. "What must I *do* to inherit eternal life?" (v. 17, emphasis added). His query is based on the assumption that eternal life is at the end of *doing* rather than the result of *being*. There is a sort of elitist presumption here that the gifted or wealthy have the inside track to what's best in religion or, as this man puts it, "eternal life."

So Jesus gave him a list of things to do—keep the commandments. The man replied, "All these I have kept since I was a boy" (v. 20). The rabbis taught that the Law could be kept in its entirety. Even the apostle Paul said of his days before he became a Christian that his life in relation to legalistic righteousness was faultless (see Philippians 3:6). It's fair to note that though Jesus considered the man's claim superficial, it would not have been considered preposterous by the man's friends and neighbors.

Jesus' response suggests that He agreed with the man and gave him some more things to do, but they are not additions to the original list. If the phrase, "do not defraud," refers to the 10th commandment, we have in verse 19 a listing of the final six of the Ten Commandments, which all prohibit wrong actions against other people. The first four commandments discuss our relationship with God; and it was there, in an area of life much more personal and inward than the other commands, that the rich young man was lacking.

All of Christ's demands in this story grow out of His love for the man and His understanding of the Kingdom. Jesus said to the rich young ruler, "Go, sell everything you have and give to the poor, and you will have treasure in heaven. Then come, follow me" (v. 21). When the rich young man asked Jesus what he needed to do in order to inherit eternal life, he was thinking in terms of what he could do to earn his way to heaven and to righteousness, while Jesus tried to tell him that a right relationship with God is a gift to be received.

"At this the man's face fell. He went away sad, because he had great wealth" (v. 22). He was sad, but he still went away. Jesus had placed the standard so high the disciples nearly went into shock, which brings us to what we might call in our day . . .

Tough Luck

We understand "tough love," at least in some situations. We expect a parent to take a dangerous toy from a child, even if the child screams, "You don't love me!" We applaud the parent who sets limits for teen behavior, even though the teen rebels at the boundaries. Tough love is unconditional but not unqualified. Tough love says, "I love you so much you cannot do anything that would keep me from loving you." However, tough love also says, "Because I love you so much, I will make demands on you that I would never impose on a casual acquaintance."

It was the tough love of Jesus that said, "Go, sell . . . then come, follow."

I remember when the banker came to our church. Our church was impoverished, ignored, located in the "wrong" part of town. Then the banker came to church. The graybeards in our congregation talked about how wonderful it would be if the banker were a member of our church. "Finally, the town would know we're here," they said. But the banker never returned. That was tough. Some would say that it was "tough luck."

Surely there was some of that in the disciples' reaction when the rich man chose not to meet the demands of Christ's tough love. They were so close to having an influential, wealthy person join them. But he left. That was tough. Tough luck!

Yet, there is more to the disciples' question, "Who then can be saved?" (v. 26). Far more than lost status, their inquiry reveals their concern about their own future. Peter caught the heartbeat of the group when he said, "We have left everything to follow you!" (v. 28). We know how to translate this concern. If the man who had everything couldn't make it, what's going to happen to us? And don't forget, Lord, we've given up all we have to follow You.

Jesus created the dilemma for the disciples because He told a story. When the rich young ruler left, Jesus talked about a camel and the eye of a needle. Some have proposed that there was a gate in the city wall called the Needle's Gate, a gate so small a camel would have to be unloaded and forced to crawl through on its knees. A beautiful picture speaking of humbleness and the full release of our possessions.

Still, could a camel go through the eye of this needle? Yes, say some. "It's possible for a camel to go through the eye of a needle," C. S. Lewis said, "but it would be extremely hard on the camel."

There appears to be more to Jesus' words than this example shows. Perhaps Jesus was really thinking about a camel
and an actual eye of a tailor's needle. Now that is sheer impossibility. And that is exactly Jesus' point.

Jesus' words run contrary to the human spirit, which
thinks surely there is something we can do to earn our salvation. Yet, Jesus said, "Apart from me you can do nothing"
(John 15:5). Concerning the salvation of all of us, not just
the rich man, Jesus said to the disciples, "With man this is
impossible, but not with God; all things are possible with
God" (Mark 10:27). No one can inherit eternal life because
of anything they own or do. In the camel story, the exaggera-
tion emphasizes the impossibility.

Still, we are more often like the man walking the spirited
St. Bernard. I saw such a man in the park one day and wondered who was walking whom. Was the man taking the dog
for a walk or the dog leading the man? Seemed to me like the
dog was in charge—and knew it.

Did the wealthy man own his possessions? Or did they
own him? The burden of possessions, small or great, is a lot
like walking a St. Bernard.

R. H. Gundry said, "That Jesus did not command all his
followers to sell all their possessions gives comfort only to the
kind of people to whom he would issue that command."[2] If
that's true, the question is still open. To whom would Jesus
have issued the command?

In our humanness, we are tempted to limit this hard word
from Jesus to the very rich. Francis of Assisi responded to the
challenge of this passage by renouncing his family's wealth.
The New Testament as a whole, however, does not require
this of all. Wealthy people, such as Lydia (Acts 16:14),
Phoebe (Romans 16:1-2), Priscilla and Aquila (Romans 16:3-
5), and Gaius (Romans 16:23), played a very important role
in the spread of the gospel by making their spacious homes
available for Christian gatherings. More important than the
renunciation of wealth itself, Mark's story teaches, is the re-

nunciation of the attitudes characteristic of the world of the wealthy. Ultimately if we listen to God's Word, we'll see that, while the demands of discipleship will vary from individual to individual, discipleship takes on the form of the cross for every believer.

Nothing less than a willingness to give everything to Jesus will ever meet the Master's demands. The joyous truth, however, in regard to our salvation is that "what is impossible with men is possible with God" (Luke 18:27). So the question for all of us becomes a matter of where we put our trust, in what we have and can do or in Jesus. Or as the martyred missionary Jim Elliot wrote in his diary more than a half century ago, "He is no fool who gives up what he cannot keep to gain what he cannot lose."

Notes:

1. Hayim Hahman Bialik and Yehoshua Hana Ravnitsky, eds., *The Book of Legends* (New York: Shocken Books, 1992), 601.

2. R. T. France, *The Gospel of Matthew* (Leicester, Eng.: InterVarsity Press, 1985), 286.

THE DIFFICULT WORDS:

Take your pay and go. I want to give the man who was hired last the same as I gave you. Don't I have the right to do what I want with my own money? Or are you envious because I am generous? (Matthew 20:14-15).

BACKGROUND SCRIPTURE: Matthew 20:1-16

TRUTH TO REMEMBER:

God is gracious to everyone, beyond merit or expectation.

GUIDANCE ALONG OUR JOURNEY:

In the kingdom of God, the values of the world are turned topsy-turvy. Humility is valued more than pride; dependence and trust more than autonomy and self-reliance; sacrificial giving more than materialism. When compared to the ways of the world, the kingdom of God is an entirely different way of seeing things. And it is dramatically different from the perceptions of our culture.

The parable of the vineyard turns things around. The last will be first and the first will be last. Those who have worked all day will be paid the same as those who have worked an hour. At first, this seems unfair. But when we read the account closely, we find that there was an agreement and there were promises. In reality, the parable of the vineyard is not about fairness; it is about the generosity of the landowner. Since the landowner represents God, he serves to remind us of God's gracious dealings with us.

This is the fifth chapter of our study of hard sayings we find in the New Testament. Some of the sayings are hard to hear because they are hard to do. They call Christ's followers to a costly way of life. Other sayings are called "hard" because they are difficult to understand. The focus for this chapter falls into the latter category. When people hear the saying now, it is easy to miss the point that Jesus was making then.

This chapter helps us to see that God treats everyone, not only with justice and fairness but also with generosity. His generosity to some does not imply that He is treating others unfairly. Consequently, this account should prompt us to give thanks to God for His justice and His grace. He does "what is right" and goes far beyond what could be expected.

Chapter 5

A Fair Rate for the Job

ALL THE MAN SAID was, "I'd sure like to go back to the good old days when life was easier."

His friend exploded. "Let me tell you about the good old days!" the friend replied. "In 1937 or '38, southern California had an extremely cold winter. Orange growers knew they had lost their crop and were afraid they would lose their trees too. So they hired men to keep the smudge pots[1] burning 24 hours a day."

The man continued, "My father was one of the men hired to keep the smudge pots burning. He worked 18 to 20 hours a day for two straight weeks. By then his lungs were so full of oily smoke he became ill and took a day off work. When he returned the next day, he was fired because he 'wasn't reliable.'" With more fire in his eye than there had been in the smudge pots, the son said, "Don't talk to me about the 'good old days.' They never were that good!"

The story about the man and the smudge pots tells us volumes about the changed attitude between owners and workers since the 1930s. However, if we use it as a reference to understand this parable, we'll completely miss Christ's point. This hard word from Jesus is not about labor-management relations, as crucial as they are and as vital as it is for workers and owners to be ethical as they work together. It does, however, give us another glimpse of who God is. What we see immediately places our human outlook on life in tension with that of the Lord's. So let's take a closer look at the meaning of Jesus' words when He said, "Take your pay and go. I want to give

the man who was hired last the same as I gave you. Don't I
have the right to do what I want with my own money? Or are
you envious because I am generous?" (Matthew 20:14-15).

The Human Side

How much weight can three letters carry? We'll need to
explore the dimensions of that question as we work toward an
understanding of what Jesus said—a hard saying that begins
with these words from Matthew, "*For* the kingdom of heaven
is like a landowner who went out early in the morning to hire
men to work in his vineyard" (20:1, emphasis added).

Without immersing ourselves in an English lesson, it's important to note that the word "for" is a conjunction—a word
that connects two sentences or two ideas together. It's like a
bridge over which we travel from one idea to the next, bringing along all the meaning of the first concept. Or, in this case,
since we're already beyond the bridge, we need to travel back
across it to see what has been left behind.

The word "for" takes us back to Matthew 19:30, "But
many who are first will be last, and many who are last will be
first." That verse forces us to look again at the disciples' response to the departure of the rich young ruler. A man who
had everything, including the money to buy anything, chose
not to become a disciple of Jesus because the price was too
high. The astonished disciples asked, "Who then can be
saved?" (19:25).

The disciples were clearly dissatisfied with our Lord's answer, for Peter lamented, "We have left everything to follow
you! What then will there be for us?" (19:27). The conversation that followed prompted Jesus to say something like this,
"Since all this is true, let me tell you a story." Then He relat-
ed one of the most difficult to accept of all the Gospel parables—the parable of the workers in the vineyard.

Jesus' story was true-to-life. In New Testament times, un-
employment in Palestine was quite high. In some places at

various times, 50 percent of adult males could not find work. They looked to the day-labor market for survival. These unemployed men gathered at dawn at a central location, to which owners would go to hire as many laborers as they needed for the day. The prevailing wage for day-workers was one *denarius*, which, according to the Law, had to be paid at the end of the day. Workers desperately needed the money, for it took about a *denarius* a day for a family to subsist.

Up to that point, Jesus' story created no problems. The disciples had seen this drama played out in their towns morning after morning. In fact, since some of them were businessmen before they chose to follow Jesus, they may have hired day laborers in the same way. Nor would they have been surprised when the owner went to the labor pool to hire more men before the day was over. At harvest, crops must be gathered quickly, lest a year's work be destroyed by a few minutes of violent weather.

Then, at the end of the day after the work was done, the "storm" hit. The landowner chose to pay each worker a single *denarius*, whether he had worked one hour or all day. Having waited while everyone else was paid, those who started first obviously expected to be paid more than their original contract with the landowner. There were smaller coins than *denarii*. The latecomers could have been given a coin of smaller value, reflecting their lesser contribution to the harvest. Since they were paid a *denarius* for less than a full day's work, the full-dayers expected more.

At this point, it might be revealing to pause and reflect about which people have our sympathy in this story. The landowner? The early workers? The last to be hired? Probably, most of us identify with those who worked all day and were given only one *denarius*. It wasn't fair. After all, we keep insisting, life must be fair. Tragically, there's not much mercy in our self-serving logic.

It's nearly impossible for us not to make this a sociological study—a study in poor labor relations. However, this story is not about how much each worker earned or was paid. This story is about God. For that reason, let's turn to the divine side of this parable.

The Divine Side

In our haste to correct the injustice in this story, we are tempted to rush by the opening phrase of the parable, "For the kingdom of heaven is like" (20:1). R. T. France says, "We might paraphrase these words by saying, 'This is what it is like when God is at work.'"[2]

A quick look at another parable Jesus told about the kingdom of heaven illustrates this point. "The kingdom of heaven is like a mustard seed, which a man took and planted in his field" (Matthew 13:31). The kingdom of heaven is not compared to the seed itself but to what happens after it is sown. Jesus was saying something like this, "When God is at work, it's like the miracle of the tiny mustard seed that grows into a large plant." The emphasis is not on what the mustard seed is, but what happens after it is planted. So also this parable.

The question we are tempted to ask is, "Why wasn't the employer fair?" The better question is, "In what way does the landowner illustrate the way God works?" These words provide both warning and hope. A warning lest people think they can earn their way into the Kingdom by the value of the gift they give, the costliness of their sacrifice, or the length of their service. The hope is found in discovering more about who God is. Let's turn in that direction in our study.

God is sovereign. Most of us don't use the word "sovereign" very often in our daily conversation. We are more familiar with democratically elected officials, who have limited power delegated to them by a constitution. In the sense in which the word is applied to God, a sovereign is a person who has unlimited, absolute, supreme power over everything and everyone.

God is revealed in this parable as sovereign. Note how the

sovereign God speaks in the words of the landowner, "Don't I have the right to do what I want with my own money?" (v. 15). Our reaction might be, "Of course, not. There are written and unwritten rules of conduct that we all know and live by. Besides, it's not fair." Yet, God is not an elected head of state. He is sovereign and thus is under no obligation to anyone, not even those who regulate fair employment practices.

The kingdom of heaven is unlike any other kingdom. Few leaders in the history of the world have had undiluted power. Even despotic evil men like Adolf Hitler and Joseph Stalin have lacked total control. They became dictators by means of intrigue and manipulation. They remained in power only through violence and conspiracy.

However, God did not arrive at His exalted position by overthrowing some existing god or gods in a cosmic battle. God is, always has been, and always will be the Sovereign of the universe.

Nor is God an evil conspirator on the world scene. In fact, if God were evil, this parable would carry a devastating message. This is the God of the parable of the prodigal son, where the Father (God) gives to each son according to his need. This is the God who, while dying as a human on the center cross, turned to one thief and said, "Today you will be with me in paradise" (Luke 23:43). There would be no waiting in an outer room until the thief had "enough time in grade," as they say in the military.

Thus, it is demonstrated again that His kingdom is different from those we know in our world. Matthew presents 10 parables that have become known as "Kingdom parables." In them, he doesn't present details and events concerning the Kingdom, but defines the mission of Jesus to establish God as king. Which is another way of saying, "This is what it will be like when God is in control."

The God described in the parable of the workers in the vineyard is a God of grace. Hear the central message of this hard saying from Jesus: God is not bound by traditions and cultural norms, nor can He act only in ways humans judge to be fair. That's what makes this story a gracious word. He gives to each of us according to our need. The family of the man who had to wait until 5 P.M. before he was hired was just as hungry as the family of the man hired at 6 A.M. Neither could survive on less than a *denarius* a day.

God's generosity transcends all human ideas of fairness. If that were not true, then none of us would ever know the power of His redeeming grace. None of us deserve His forgiveness, nor could any of us set aside enough credits from our good deeds to buy a ticket into heaven. This parable stresses that God is in debt to no one. Thus, every gift from Him is an extension of His grace, so that no one receives less than he or she needs nor as much as his or her greed might demand.

Still, we ask, "Doesn't God reward those who are faithful to Him?" Yes, of course, He does. But not as we measure reward. One of the better answers to this question is found in a prayer that comes to us from the 16th century, "Teach us to labor and not to ask for any reward save that of knowing that we do Thy will."[3]

Notes:

1. Smudge pots, used to heat orange groves, were simple stoves that burned crude oil. The pots belched out black, dense, oily smoke. Sometimes, during extended cold periods, the air pollution near the groves would be so great that drivers would have to turn on their headlights at midday. Smudge pots are no longer legal. Orchard heaters are now used.

2. R. T. France, *The Gospel According to Matthew* (Leicester, Eng.: Inter-Varsity Press, 1985), 225.

3. Charles L. Allen, *When the Heart Is Hungry* (Fleming H. Revell Co., 1965), 144.

THE DIFFICULT WORDS:
Many are invited, but few are chosen (Matthew 22:14).

BACKGROUND SCRIPTURE: Matthew 22:1-14

TRUTH TO REMEMBER:
To be included in God's covenant community, people must respond properly to His invitation to be a disciple.

GUIDANCE ALONG OUR JOURNEY:
The **BACKGROUND SCRIPTURE** for this chapter (Matthew 22:1-14) is referred to as the parable of the wedding banquet. In order for this parable to make any sense at all, we must understand two things:

First, the invitation from the king is an invitation to a feast—a celebration. This is a Kingdom parable. And Jesus says that the kingdom of heaven can be compared to a royal wedding feast. It is the King's desire for us to join Him in celebrating His joy.

The second thing that must be understood has to do with the difference between the invited and the chosen. The difference between them lies in their response to the invitation. It has to do with the matter of personal choice. The ones who were not chosen were invited, but it was their choice not to respond. The King's invitation has been extended, and every person has a choice to make.

Chapter 6

FEW ARE CHOSEN

HOW DO YOU SUPPOSE people would react if a professor with a Ph.D. in economics were to say to a student in her class on international banking, "Mommy wants to count your itsy bitsy toes"?

I suspect we'd either conclude that she is bonkers and call the people in the white coats, or decide she is not morally fit to work with young people and call someone with a badge. However, if she were talking to her baby, we'd accept the conversation as perfectly normal, even for someone with her academic credentials.

What's the difference? Not the speaker. Nor the words. They are the same. The difference is the audience. Often, as with the professor, the message cannot be understood without knowing the person or persons to whom the words are directed. Otherwise the words can be easily misunderstood, sometimes with devastating effect.

That's the situation we face today when we hear Jesus say, "For many are called, but few are chosen" (Matthew 22:14, NASB).

The fact that these words are difficult to understand has been well documented in the history of Christian thought. The meaning of the saying is best understood when interpreted within the context of the passage in which it appears.

Jesus compared the coming of the kingdom of heaven to a wedding feast. It was customary for guests of such a special occasion to be formally invited well in advance. Then, on the day when the festivities were to begin, last-minute reminders would be given to those who had been invited. This means that those who rejected the invitation in the parable had already been given plenty of opportunity to send any legitimate "regrets." So their refusal represented a serious affront to the king.

The parable pictures the messianic wedding banquet. The king represents God, and the king's son is Christ. The invited guests are the Jews who claimed to be anticipating the coming of the Messiah. The Gentiles are those who were urged to come from the streets to fill the wedding hall. The killing of the messengers represents the persecution of those who proclaim Christ's message. The destruction and burning of their city is considered by some scholars as a veiled reference to the future destruction of Jerusalem in A.D. 70.

The king's actions toward the man who was not properly attired would seem to be rather harsh when you consider that he was hustled right off the streets and into the banquet hall. However, some authorities have suggested that the king would have provided the guests with wedding garments for a royal wedding, so that his failure to show the proper respect was inexcusable. Regardless of the custom, the implication is that the man's soiled garments were unacceptable because they were an insult to the king. The new life of the believer is often symbolized in the New Testament by the wearing of new or unsoiled clothing (Romans 13:12-14; Galatians 3:26-27; Colossians 3:12; Revelation 3:4; 19:8). The believer's life is expected to give evidence of Christ's presence.

In this context, the hard saying at the close of the parable takes on meaning: The ones not chosen find themselves in the place of loss, not because they were omitted from the guest list but because they did not choose to accept the invitation. And those who claim to be part of the Kingdom without experiencing Christ within are only fooling themselves.

Across the years, this "hard saying" from Jesus has been misused, abused, and revised in a variety of ways. Let's note some of them.

Young men arrived outside the coach's office at least an hour before classes were to begin that morning. At precisely

7:30, the coach appeared, carrying the list of the players who had made the varsity basketball team. Moving quickly, he taped the paper to the brick wall and retreated inside his office.

Soon there were shouts of joy from the guys who made the varsity team and groans of distress from those who didn't. Those who would be playing on the junior varsity were not comforted by the words the coach wrote across the bottom of the page, "Many are called, but few are chosen."

A visitor to a tomato cannery was shown the line where employees picked out over-ripe tomatoes and threw them away. Before he left, the guide shared a tired joke with the visitor, "A few are culled, but many are chosen."

The cartoon pictured a small group of short-sleeved people huddled together in the snow for warmth. The punch line read, "Many are cold, but few are frozen."

In the aftermath of the Protestant Reformation, a theological system was developed in line with what some believed was the general teaching of this and other biblical passages. According to its proponents, some people were elected to be saved while others were elected to be damned. The choice was God's alone. It was, they suggested, a fulfillment of Christ's words when He said, "Many are called, but few are chosen."

As we have noted, some poor puns and some even poorer theology has come from these words. Our task in this chapter is to dig through the debris to discover, as much as we can, what Jesus meant when He said, "Many are invited, but few are chosen." We'll begin by taking the long view. Then, we'll zoom in on the action that preceded these words, after which we'll look at the words themselves.

The Long Story

Jesus did not wander through life as an entertainer, like a juggler at a Renaissance festival. That's a perfectly honorable occupation, but it wasn't Jesus' mission. Though to be sure, His public life was bracketed by the temptation to capture the attention and loyalty of the people through "magic." At the beginning, the devil challenged our Lord to throw himself off the roof of the Temple, claiming He would be caught by the angels and brought safely to earth (see Matthew 4:6). What a crowd-pleaser that would have been! At the end, He heard the religious authorities mock Him with the words, "Let him come down now from the cross, and we will believe in him" (27:42).

From the beginning, Jesus was totally immersed in the task of redemption. And almost from the start, Jesus was embroiled in the controversy that ultimately led to His death. In Mark's account, the conflict begins right away—in chapter 2. That's right, chapter 2.

Mark tells five stories of conflict, beginning with Christ's healing of a man in the synagogue on the Sabbath (2:1—3:6). At that point so early in His ministry, Jesus effectively signed His death warrant. His "transgression" of healing on the Sabbath was judged to be extremely serious. When He demonstrated the power to forgive sin by saying to the paralytic, "Get up, take up your mat and go home" (2:11), He crossed the line forever. Earlier He had asked the religious leaders, "Which is easier: to say to the paralytic, 'Your sins are forgiven,' or to say, 'Get up, take your mat and walk'?" (2:9). They clearly understood that He was saying, "*You* can't do either, but *I* can do both." His claim to be God could not be, and was not, tolerated by the opposition.

So, they decided to kill Him. At the end of the last of the five conflict stories early in Mark's Gospel, the account says, "Then the Pharisees went out and began to plot with the Herodians how they might kill Jesus" (3:6). What a combination! The Pharisees were the most highly respected and considered to be the most devout religious people in the land. And the Herodians were the members of the business community who cooperated with Rome, the hated conquerors of their country.

Both the Pharisees and the Herodians had a lot to lose if Jesus continued His revolutionary teachings. From their point of view, He had to be stopped. It was a matter of *when* and *how*, not *if* and *maybe*.

That's the long story, of which this chapter's biblical focus is almost the final chapter.

The Short Story

The events surrounding the parable of the wedding banquet took place on Tuesday of Jesus' final week on earth. However, if we are to understand them, we need to go back to the previous Sunday. On that day, Jesus entered Jerusalem on a young donkey. We know it as the Triumphal Entry and celebrate it on Palm Sunday. All the Gospels report the story.

Jesus may have visited the Temple briefly on Sunday afternoon, but the real action came on Monday when he "cleansed" the Temple. He disrupted what had become a corrupt and profitable business of selling animals for sacrifice. Then, He announced, "It is written, . . . 'My house will be called a house of prayer,' but you are making it a 'den of robbers'" (Matthew 21:13). Jesus then returned to Bethany to spend Tuesday night.

On Wednesday, Jesus was challenged by the religious leaders when He entered the Temple courts. The chief priests and teachers of the Law were angry because of what Jesus had said the day before. Now in earnest, they "began looking for a way to kill him, for they feared him, because the whole crowd was amazed at his teaching" (Mark 11:18). The need to kill had become intense. Only the crowd held them back.

In that volatile atmosphere needing only a spark to ignite it, Jesus told three stories, of which this chapter's Bible focus is the last. Both the crowd and the religious leaders knew that the stories Jesus told were designed to reveal the hypocrisy of those who controlled the Temple and their ancient traditions.

At the conclusion of the first story, Jesus said to the leaders who opposed Him, "The tax collectors and the prostitutes are entering the kingdom of God ahead of you" (Matthew

21:32). Then, Jesus told a story about some tenant farmers who killed the owner's son so they could grab the property. Looking into His accusers eyes, He said, "I tell you that the kingdom of God will be taken away from you and given to a people who will produce its fruit" (21:43). Is it any wonder that Matthew reports, "When the chief priests and the Pharisees heard Jesus' parables, they knew he was talking about them. [So] they looked for a way to arrest him" (21:45-46)?

The Inside Story

Perhaps it would be more correct to say, "This is how it looks from inside the story." Note the vital words Jesus used at the beginning of the story we know as the parable of the wedding banquet. Jesus said, "*The kingdom of heaven is like* a king who prepared a wedding banquet for his son" (Matthew 22:2, emphasis added).

This is a Kingdom parable. Unless we keep this in plain sight at all times, the parable cannot be understood, and the final words of Jesus lose their meaning. This Kingdom parable's immediate target was the religious leaders. Beyond them, the covenant people are implicated because they had concluded that their special position with God made them privileged people on earth.

They casually rejected a grand offer. Both leaders and people had exchanged the opportunity to serve others with the conclusion that they deserved to be served. They had, as a people, rejected God's invitation. As those who received the second call to the wedding banquet, these people made a decision not to respond to the invitation. If Matthew were writing today, he might have had the people say, "I'm too busy." Still, whether they "shrugged their shoulders and went off" (TM), "laughed" (TLB), or "made light of it and went away" (NRSV), it was clearly a deliberate rejection of a grand offer.

Obeying the tyranny of money, they "went off—one to his field, another to his business" (v. 5). Keep in mind that this is not a textbook on economics, but a Kingdom parable. Instead of being honored, they not only rejected the invitation, they killed the messengers. Remember the scene in the Temple where these words were spoken. Jesus, challenged by the religious leaders, responded with this story. Those who listened were, at that moment, seeking to find a way to kill the one speaking to them. They had to get rid of Him lest He hurt the economy and bankrupt them in the process.

We were there too. The clear message of Jesus in the Temple is that, because the covenant people and their leaders had rejected the message, the invitation would be broadened to all people. The king instructed his servants to "invite to the banquet anyone you find" (v. 9). We are among those the servants found.

Now the story gets tough for us. Up to now, the challenge had been directed to the covenant people, but that changes with the wider invitation. The religious leaders failed to lead the people into an authentic relationship with God. This led God to establish a new covenant community.

Among those who arrived for the banquet was one who showed so little respect for the king he didn't dress properly. Even though this man was invited from the streets, his failure to take it seriously was an insult to the host.

God, said Jesus, was in the process of establishing a new covenant community. Yet, there would be no free passes for the "street people"—the Gentiles and sinners. Though they were invited, they were not welcome unless and until they were willing to change and be changed. As William Barclay writes, "Grace is not only a gift; grace is a grave responsibility. A man cannot go on living the life he lived before he met Jesus Christ. He must be clothed in a new purity, a new holiness and a new goodness."*

Thus Jesus said, "Many are invited, but few are chosen" (v. 14). To be "invited," as used by Matthew here, is to be one who has accepted the invitation to become a guest or member of a select group—God's people. To be "chosen" identifies those who respond positively to the privileges of God's grace and trust in Him for salvation. They become a part of the community of believers.

The "hard saying" will not go away as much as we might like it to disappear. The first guests insulted the king by refusing to come when invited; the second offended him by refusing to prepare himself properly for the banquet. We have the opportunity to change the pattern and respond in a way that pleases the King.

---

*William Barclay, *The Gospel of Matthew* (Philadelphia: The Westminster Press, 1958), II:298.

THE DIFFICULT WORDS:

My God, my God, why have you forsaken me? (Matthew 27:46b).

BACKGROUND SCRIPTURE: Matthew 27:32-50

TRUTH TO REMEMBER:

In the midst of any Christian's darkest hour, there is yet reason to hope.

GUIDANCE ALONG OUR JOURNEY:

Jesus had been suffering the agony of the Cross for about six hours when He cried out, "My God, my God, why have you forsaken me?" In these words, we discover the real torment of the Cross. He coped with the humiliation of being arrested and falsely accused. He tolerated the ridicule and jeers from the onlookers. He endured the physical pain of crucifixion to the point of death.

Yet, what caused Him to cry out in deepest grief was the consequence of bearing our sin for us and the feeling of utter abandonment that came with that act of love.

This chapter moves right to the heart of the gospel. We will take a painful look at the price that was paid for our salvation. For Christ, it was the greatest price that could be paid. And the familiar words of John 3:16 remind us that it was no less for God the Father.

Still, in the midst of grief and loneliness, Jesus reminds us of something that may escape the casual reader of the Gospels. At His greatest point of need, there was yet reason to hope. We need to be reminded about the wages of sin. The cost is separation from God and death. We also need to be reminded that Jesus has endured anything and everything that could possibly come our way. By His example, we can learn in our darkest hour to cry out to our Heavenly Father, who hears, cares, and responds.

Chapter 7

"WHY HAVE YOU FORSAKEN ME?"

AFTER DARK on the night of October 16, 1860, John Brown and a few comrades occupied the United States armory in Harper's Ferry, Virginia. Called by historians a wolf-like, menacing, brooding figure who compared himself with Christ, Brown hoped to ignite a slave rebellion in the southern United States. A small detachment of marines led by Colonel Robert E. Lee captured Brown a few hours later. The state of Virginia tried and convicted Brown of treason, murder, and fomenting insurrection. When his brother begged him to plead insanity to avoid a death penalty, he said, "I am worth inconceivably more to hang than for any other purpose." He died on the scaffold December 2, 1860.

The power and influence of this strange and troubled man lived on. He became a hero to some northern antislavery leaders. They printed and distributed the speech he made just before his sentencing. In it, he said in part:

> If it is deemed necessary that I should forfeit my life for the furtherance of the ends of justice, and mingle my blood with the blood of my children and with the blood of millions in this slave country whose rights are disregarded by wicked, cruel, and unjust enactments, I say, let it be done.[1]

People who consider themselves martyrs talk like that.

Nathan Hale, schoolteacher and captain in the Continental Army during the American Revolution against Great Britain, was captured and executed because he was a spy. His final words, part of the heroic literature of the United States, were, "I only regret that I have but one life to lose for my country."[2]

Polycarp, bishop of Smyrna, was executed in A.D. 155. Alerted that he would be arrested, Polycarp chose to wait for the soldiers rather than leave the city. The Roman proconsul gave him the choice of cursing the name of Christ and making a sacrifice to Caesar or death. Polycarp replied, "Eighty and six years have I served Him [Christ] and He has done me no wrong. How can I blaspheme my King who saved me?"[3]

Martyrs are like that. They go to their deaths convinced of the rightness of their cause and confident that the future will justify their actions.

Yet on the Cross, Jesus "cried out in a loud voice, . . . 'My God, my God, why have you forsaken me?'" (Matthew 27:46). Most of us have neither the courage nor the need to become martyrs. Still, we understand them—at least a little. We may admire or despise their message, but we cannot escape the power of their dedication to a cause—a cause for which they are willing to die.

However, Jesus was not a martyr; He was the Savior. His words on the Cross reveal dimensions of experience we cannot imagine, describe, or define. Yet, we cannot dodge them. Though we can only tug at the edges of this riddle, we must seek to find some meaning in it, for these words contain not only the mystery but also the magnificence of the Cross.

My God, Why?

We understand this question because we've asked it often. In times of sorrow and personal loss. In times of despair and failure. When all we counted sacred has been trampled in the mud. When those we confided in have betrayed us, we ask "Why?" Many expand the question to, "My God, why?" It's a question as old as Job and as fresh as this morning's life-changing, bad-news phone call.

It should not surprise us if Jesus expressed some very human emotions while He was being crucified. Or, to put it another way, we will only be surprised if we conclude that God, not the God-Man, hung on the Cross. The apostle Paul reminded the believers in Philippi that "though he [Jesus] was in the form of God, [he] did not regard equality with God as something to be exploited, but emptied himself, taking the form of a slave, being born in human likeness" (Philippians 2:6-7, NRSV). Whatever else the coming together of God and man in Bethlehem's cattle stall may teach us, it certainly means that, at the end, the One who died on a cross suffered as a human.

The picturesque language of *The Message* captures the same idea when it tells us that "The Word [Jesus] became flesh and blood and moved into the neighborhood" (John 1:14). As a man, Jesus showed a wide range of human emotion and participated fully in the human experience. He became tired and hungry, as did the disciples—and no one questions their humanity. He expressed a very human love to His mother from the Cross. Why, then, should it surprise us if He were to ask the question we, too, have asked, "Why?"

Nevertheless, this man's death was unlike any other who died on a cross. At midday on that famous Friday, the darkness of night fell on the land. For three hours, the people were shrouded by what the ancients believed was a symbol of God's displeasure. Darkness had signified judgment in the past and would in the future. Eight centuries earlier, the prophet Amos spoke of a time when God would actively intervene in history, primarily for judgment. He asked, "Why do you long for the day of the LORD? That day will be darkness, not light" (5:18). Zephaniah identified it as the day when "the LORD's wrath comes upon you" (2:2).

Thus, we must look beyond that which is strictly human as we tug at the edges of this great riddle.

My God, Why Have You Abandoned Me?

The traditional wedding ceremony includes these words, "Forsaking all others [will you] keep yourself only unto her [or him] as long as you both shall live?" We know that these words of commitment are a promise to absolute purity in sexual conduct. When we agree to them, we enter into a covenant to exclude any and all others from the intimacy that is at the center of marriage. We abandon all others for just one person.

"Abandon" captures the full force of the word Jesus spoke from the Cross. Outside the marriage ceremony, we don't use the word "forsake" very often. However, we understand the word "abandon." We talk about abandoned children and see the hopelessness in their eyes. We speak of abandoned buildings and note the emptiness. We hear of an abandoned ship and picture a vessel with neither owner nor destination and likely no future. We hear the flat, forlorn words of an abandoned spouse. Some of us have known times when we felt cut off from God, when it seemed as though our prayers bounced off the ceiling. Or as the pioneers in the faith used to say, "The heavens were brass." "Abandon" is a part of our vocabulary.

When Jesus cried out in a loud voice, "My God, my God, why have you abandoned me?" (Matthew 27:46, TM), He seems to have experienced a divine desertion. Is it possible for us to understand these words from Christ?

Often the Bible is the best commentary on the Bible. That would seem to be the situation here. Let's begin our journey of discovery in the Book of Hebrews, where the writer demonstrates how Jesus became the extension and fulfillment of the work of the high priests. Those priests served as a bridge between earth and heaven, between sinful humanity and a holy God.

Among the ritual duties performed by the priests was the offering of sacrifices to God for the sins of the people. "But," says the writer to the Hebrews, "those sacrifices are an annual reminder of sins" (10:3). In other words, they could remind the people that they were sinners but brought no hope of deliverance from sin in the future.

However, the writer declares, "We have a great high priest who has gone through the heavens, Jesus the Son of God" (4:14). The good news continues, "When this priest had offered for all time one sacrifice for sins, he sat down at the right hand of God" (10:12). Ah, but there is more! This high priest "is [able] to sympathize with our weaknesses, . . . [because He] has been tempted in every way, just as we are—*yet was without sin*" (4:15, emphasis added).

The writer to the Hebrews explains how Jesus became our Redeemer, "Since the children"—that's you and me, and the people of all ages—"have flesh and blood, he too shared in their humanity so that by his death he might destroy him who holds the power of death—that is, the devil—and free those who all their lives were held in slavery by their fear of death" (2:14-15).

At this point, it may help us to see this from a different angle. Let's look at it as viewed by the apostle Paul. He wrote, "God made him [Jesus] who had no sin to be sin for us, so that in him we might become the righteousness of God" (2 Corinthians 5:21). These words bring us closer to the darkness that was thrown like a shroud over Calvary. A darkness that was pierced by a loud cry of abandonment.

At the center of the mystery of Calvary are these words, "God made him who had no sin to be sin for us." "Up to this moment," writes William Barclay, "Jesus had gone through every experience of life except one—He had never known the consequence of sin. Now if there is one thing sin does, . . . it separates us from God. . . . In this terrible, grim, bleak moment, Jesus truly identified himself with the sin of man."[4]

At the heart of the story of the Cross is a sense of failure. The One who had come to save the world was dying with the world unsaved. His friends had scattered; no one understood why He chose to allow himself to be executed. All they could see was a shattered dream.

Yet here, also, is the magnificence of the Cross. A closer

examination of Christ's final week in Jerusalem reveals that He was not the victim; He was in control of His destiny. In Gethsemane, He battled the temptation to find an easier way. Then, having chosen to follow the will of the Father, He waited for Judas and the soldiers to arrive. The night that allowed the disciples to flee would have protected Him also. Yet, He chose to die for our sins. Earlier He had said, "I lay down my life—only to take it up again. No one takes it from me, but I lay it down of my own accord" (John 10:17-18).

Many of those who watched Jesus on the Cross challenged Him to save himself and come down off the Cross. "Let him come down now from the cross, and we will believe in him" (Matthew 27:42). However, it is actually because He would *not* come down that He became our Savior. The Jews only visualized a powerful messiah; God's Messiah was characterized instead by sacrificial love.

The Cross was more than abandonment—it was victory. John tells us that after the terrifying cry of abandonment, Jesus said, "It is finished" (19:30). Luke tells us that, nearing completion of His redemptive work, Jesus said, "'Father, into your hands I commit my spirit.' When he had said this, he breathed his last" (23:46).

The darkness disappeared. The light returned. Hope was reborn. And with it, the confidence that the God who did not eternally abandon the Son will not desert us either. Thus, the Cross is transformed from a vehicle of terror and death to a symbol of life and joy. And so we can sing with the hymn writer,

> In the cross of Christ I glory,
> Tow'ring o'er the wrecks to time.
> All the light of sacred story
> Gathers round its head sublime.
>
> Bane and blessing, pain and pleasure
> By the Cross are sanctified;
> Peace is there that knows no measure,
> Joys that through all time abide.[5]

Notes:

1. James M. McPherson, *Battle Cry of Freedom* (New York: Oxford University Press, 1988), 209.

2. The Connecticut Society of the Sons of the American Revolution. <http://www.ctssar.org/patriots/nathan_hale.htm>. Accessed January 27, 2004.

3. Kirsopp Lake, *Martyrdom of Polycarp*. <http://www.earlychristianwritings .com/text/martyrdompolycarp-lake.html>. Accessed January 27, 2004.

4. William Barclay, *The Gospel of Mark* (Philadelphia: The Westminster Press, 1956), 383.

5. John Bowring, 1825.

THE DIFFICULT WORDS:

I tell you the truth, this generation will certainly not pass away until all these things have happened (Matthew 24:34-35).

BACKGROUND SCRIPTURE: Matthew 24:1-14, 30-35

TRUTH TO REMEMBER:

Christ's words concerning the end of the age call us to consider our personal preparation while tempering premature excitement.

GUIDANCE ALONG OUR JOURNEY:

Gethsemane and the Cross are just three short days away, and the disciples are troubled. Something is in the air! They can see that the confrontation between Jesus and the religious leaders is escalating. They know that there are people who want to kill Jesus. They do not understand the remarkable things that are occurring, like His triumphal entry into Jerusalem. And they are afraid to ask Jesus what He means when He tells them that He is going to die. These devout followers of Christ believe that what He has told them is true, but they do not understand how He can keep any of His promises if He is going to die.

As the disciples move toward the shadow of the Cross, surely they sense something of great importance is about to happen. But what? Their question about "the end of the age" represents an attempt to resolve the conflicting issues that are troubling them. As Jesus answers their questions, He deals with many of our concerns as well.

Most people have an absorbing interest in the future. It's understandable. That's where we'll spend the rest of our lives! Yet, amazingly, while we fret and stew about the future, few people spend much time preparing for it. Of course, we can't draw a blueprint of the future, because the future is by definition unknowable. What little we can know comes from the lips of Jesus. In Matthew 24, Jesus gives us an extended discussion of the "end times."

Chapter 8

THIS GENERATION SHALL
NOT PASS AWAY

IT WAS TUESDAY of Passion Week. Jesus had visited the Temple for the last time. His public ministry to the crowds was completed. He would spend the rest of His time preparing His disciples for the events that would come on Friday.

As Jesus and the disciples were leaving the Temple area, some of them expressed the awe they felt about the grandeur of the building. It is unlikely that any of them had ever seen anything to rival the beauty of Herod's Temple.

The building of the main structure of the Temple took 10 years (19—9 B.C.). However, work on the entire collection of buildings which comprised the Temple was still in progress when Jesus was there with His disciples. It took 83 years to finish building the whole complex, so that it was not completed until A.D. 64. It was constructed of white marble and plated with gold. The stones at the corners of the Temple have been found. They measure from 20 to 40 feet in length, and they weigh more than 100 tons each. No wonder the disciples remarked, "Look, Teacher! What massive stones! What magnificent buildings!" (Mark 13:1).

What is remarkable is Jesus' words of response: "Not one stone here will be left on another; every one will be thrown down" (Matthew 24:2).

That evening, the disciples were with Jesus on the Mount of Olives. They were troubled by what Jesus had said about the destruction of the Temple. The very idea was so abhorrent to them that they thought Jesus must surely be talking about the end of time. They asked Jesus a two-part question: When will this happen? What signs will tell us that it is about to happen?

Their question wrongly assumed that the destruction of the Temple would happen when Christ comes to establish His kingdom at "the end of the age." In His response, Jesus set the matter straight by distinguishing between the end of the Temple and the end of the age.

The End of the Temple: Jesus spoke of the destruction of the Temple in Matthew 24:15-25. He made specific reference to the prophecies of Daniel. In the spring of A.D. 70, Titus led his Roman troops in a siege against Jerusalem. On a late summer day, they encircled the Temple. The next day, the Temple was destroyed by fire. About 6,000 people who were seeking refuge in the Temple perished. The walls of the Temple were pulled down, and the sacred furnishings of the Temple were carried off to Rome.

The End of the Age: Jesus referred to the coming of the Son of Man at the end of time in Matthew 24:25-31. In Revelation, we are told that there will be no need for a Temple in heaven. It is "because the Lord God Almighty and the Lamb are its temple" (Revelation 21:22).

In response to their question, and with regard for their need, Jesus talked about *warnings, signs,* and *promises.*

Warnings

Jesus gave His disciples more than they asked for. They had asked for times and signs of coming events; He gave them warnings. His message was clear: Be aware and beware.

Deception: Jesus was especially concerned about those who would try to deceive His followers. In this short discourse, Jesus spoke about those deceivers in six verses (vv. 4, 5, 11, 23, 24, 26). False leaders will come teaching their own message. They will attract devoted followers. Some will perform "signs and miracles" (v. 24). Some will even make messianic claims about themselves. And three times in this passage Jesus says that they will deceive many people (vv. 5, 11, 24). The measure of any spiritual leader is the life of Christ. The question to ask, "Are people attracted to the teacher or pointed to the Christ?"

Persecution: Jesus did not say that His followers would have an easy way. He said that we would be hated because of Him. He made it clear that those who followed Him would have crosses to bear, bringing persecution, suffering, and death. When the apostles were persecuted, they rejoiced "because they had been counted worthy of suffering disgrace for the Name" (Acts 5:41).

Apostasy: The one thing most certain for every believer is change. When Christ comes into our lives, we cannot remain the same. Those who will not surrender to the changes that He calls us to make will come to hate and resent them as unreasonable or impossible demands.

Christ warns us that many will turn away. When they do, there will be betrayal and hatred. There is a twofold reason for this warning. We must be aware so we do not allow them to lead us astray. And we must beware so that we are not infected with the hatred that is associated with the feelings of betrayal.

Indifference: We are warned of the coldness that will come to characterize the lives of many who claim to be followers of Christ, "because of the increase of wickedness" (v. 12). We are warned how the distinctiveness of our witness can be compromised by our indifference toward the evil of the world. He has given us the warning so that we can avoid the natural tendency of cooling down, by fanning the embers of our concern into flame. "I remind you to fan into flame the gift of God . . . For God did not give us a spirit of timidity, but a spirit of power, of love and of self-discipline" (2 Timothy 1:6-7).

Signs

Jesus had been asked for a sign on another occasion by some of His critics, and He called them "a wicked and adulterous generation" (Matthew 12:39). However here, the question was put to Him by His most ardent followers. "What will be the sign of your coming and of the end of the age?" (v. 3).

The Beginning of Birth Pains: Jesus borrows the imagery of Jeremiah to talk about the things that people often think of as "signs" (see Jeremiah 6:24). He says that it is like the beginning of labor for a woman giving birth. Such pains will come and go over an extended period of time. He specifically names wars, rumors of wars, nation against nation, kingdom against kingdom, famines, and earthquakes. His commentary about these signs is that they are things that must happen. And even after these occurrences, we will still be waiting for the end to come. His advice: Don't be alarmed about such things.

A *Testimony to All Nations:* Proclamation of the Good News throughout the world is the assignment that Christ has given to His church. It is of such significance that our Lord declares the end will not come until it is accomplished. For the apostles who heard these words of Jesus, obedience to this directive often meant preaching to unfriendly listeners. That is why it is included with Jesus' words about persecution and apostasy. In Mark's account, this prophetic word about preaching to all nations is followed by our Lord's assurance that the Holy Spirit will enable and empower those who share this Good News.

The Sign of the Son of Man: When the disciples came to Jesus with their questions, they asked Him for a sign of His coming at the end of time. Now Jesus tells them about the coming of the Son of Man. The word He used to describe His coming is *parousia*. It is a term used for the presence, arrival, or coming of the ruler. His appearance will be sudden and clearly visible, like lightning.

At this point, Jesus told the disciples about the sign they should anticipate. "The sign of the Son of Man will appear in the sky, and all the nations of the earth will mourn. They will see the Son of Man coming on the clouds of the sky, with power and great glory" (Matthew 24:30).

On the two former occasions, when Jesus was asked to give a sign, He said, "None will be given . . . except the sign of Jonah" (Matthew 12:39; 16:4). The sign of Jonah was resurrection—from the belly of a whale for Jonah and from the bowels of the earth for Jesus Christ. Here again in 24:30, Jesus points to a sign of the resurrection.

The Lesson: Fig trees were unlike many trees in Palestine because they lost their leaves in the winter. Jesus said that when the branches begin to show signs of life, it is an indication that summer is coming. In the same way, His followers will know that the coming of the Son of Man is getting closer when they see these indicators: attempts to deceive people about Christ, persecution of believers, apostasy, indifference, the testimony of the gospel to all nations. Rather than worrying about when He is coming, we are to be ready whenever He comes.

Promises

Jesus made it clear that there will be times of great distress before the end comes. That is why He has given us the promise of His sustaining presence.

We Can Stand: Our Lord's message about the end is not one of gloom and doom; it is about salvation. "He who stands firm to the end will be saved" (v. 13). When Jesus tells us about the times of distress that will come, He says, "I have told you ahead of time" (v. 25). In Mark's account, that verse is preceded by a helpful phrase: "Be on your guard" (Mark 13:23). That is why Jesus has told us ahead of time—so that we can be on our guard, so that those things will not shake us when they come.

Heaven: When the Son of Man appears in the clouds with power and great glory, the redeemed will be gathered to be with Him in heaven. The trumpet will sound a note of victory, and the redeemed will come from the four corners of the earth.

Conclusion

The words of Jesus will stand. This world will one day be gone, but God and His truth will stand forever. This is good news! It means that we have not been left on our own; God is working for our good. It means that we are not to be overly concerned about what is coming. Because our ways are committed to Him, we can trust Him. It means that we can be ready, so that even if the worst should happen, our walk with Him will lead us right into the presence of God.

Years ago a young playwright asked Carl Sandburg to attend the performance of his play and give him advice. Sandburg went, but slept soundly throughout the entire performance. Later, the young writer complained, saying he really wanted Sandburg's opinion. Sandburg replied, "Sleep is an opinion."

And that's true! Sleep *is* an opinion. Some folks, like Rip Van Winkle, can sleep through a revolution. Some people, sadly enough, will be fast asleep—spiritually dozing—when Jesus comes. However, if we continually stay in touch with Him and constantly follow His teachings, we will be rightly prepared for His coming.

THE DIFFICULT WORDS:

Consider it pure joy, my brothers, whenever you face trials of many kinds, because you know that the testing of your faith develops perseverance (James 1:2-3).

BACKGROUND SCRIPTURE: James 1:2-18

TRUTH TO REMEMBER:

While God may test His children to strengthen their faith, He never tempts them to sin.

GUIDANCE ALONG OUR JOURNEY:

As we move through this book, it should not be surprising that some Bible passages are difficult to understand. Over 1,900 years have passed since the New Testament was written, and many cultural differences separate us from the people of the Early Church. Yet having completed eight chapters of "hard sayings," we are in a good place to look back and acknowledge that the Good News is timeless! We can give testimony that God has honored our diligent inquiry with relevant and helpful truth from His Word.

For the past eight chapters, we have focused on difficult-to-understand and difficult-to-hear sayings in the teachings of Jesus. This chapter is a turning point: Now we turn to hard sayings from other New Testament writers, beginning with one that comes to us from James.

James, the oldest of Jesus' brothers (see Matthew 13:55), is regarded as the writer of the book that bears his name. This James was recognized as a leader when the Church had a serious disagreement and discussion at Jerusalem (see Acts 15:13-21). When Peter was released from prison, he notified "James and the brothers" (12:17). When Paul went to Jerusalem, "he went to see James, and all the elders were present" (21:18). James lived as a strict Jew but demonstrated acceptance and tolerance toward Gentile Christians.

The Book of James is a letter to the Church at large about how to live the Christian life, especially when faced with great difficulties. If James could give only one word to help believers, he would say, "Persevere." Perseverance plays an important role in the Christian life. It helps us move toward mature faith. By perseverance, we learn to trust God more fully. James was concerned with the practical behavior of those who believe in Christ, so he teaches his readers how to live their faith.

Chapter 9

Is It a Test or a Temptation?

THEY WAITED UNTIL Jesus had finished His prayer. Then they asked Him, "Lord, teach us to pray" (Luke 11:1). Even now, nearly 2,000 years later, just about any believer can recite the words Jesus taught His disciples. In fact, the words pass over our lips so effortlessly that we almost fail to hear what we say. "And lead us not into temptation" (Luke 11:4).

Where did that come from? Why would Jesus teach us such a prayer? Certainly God would never lead us into temptation! How do we harmonize these words of Jesus with these words: "God cannot be tempted by evil, nor does he tempt anyone" (James 1:13)?

That is the key question to be answered in the course of this chapter, as we look closely at James 1:2-18.

Faith Perseveres Through Testing

It was probably more difficult for James to accept Jesus as Messiah than it was for others, because Jesus was His brother (see Mark 6:3; Matthew 13:55; Galatians 1:19). During the time of our Lord's ministry, James and his brothers did not seem to fully believe that Jesus was the Christ (see John 7:5). Yet, something happened that changed James completely. It may have been Christ's appearance to him after the Resurrection (see 1 Corinthians 15:7). We don't really know. However, when James became a believer, his faith changed him so thoroughly that he became a pillar of the Church (see Acts 12:17; 15:13; 21:18; Galatians 2:9).

For James, faith in Christ was a vital, life-changing experience. Faith was not so much a statement of beliefs but the lived-out expression of a changed heart. He was concerned that the life of the believer should be worthy of a profession of Jesus as the Christ. James would not be satisfied with an intellectual understanding about Jesus as Messiah. It would not be enough. James knew that faith in Christ involves both knowing Him personally and following Him daily.

Let's take a verse-by-verse look to see what James had to say about the testing of our faith.

Trials Shouldn't Kill the Joy (v. 2): In the opening of his letter, James focused on how to live a life of faith when confronted by trials and difficulties. This new life in Christ was so radically different from the perspective of the world that James's words seem at first to be somewhat unrealistic.

James was writing to a Church that had learned about persecution from experience. Throughout this letter, he referred to their trials and encouraged them to persevere. What they faced was not inconvenience for Christ's sake, but a struggle for their lives. Many believers had lost everything when they fled from their homes for safety. The Church had been scattered, so it was common for them to be separated from family and friends. Those who were not separated geographically were likely to be separated from their loved ones spiritually.

It was to this persecuted Church that James gave this advice: "Consider it pure joy whenever you face trials" (v. 2). Notice that the word "joy" did not express what he meant clearly enough. He told them to face their trials with "*pure* joy." The Greek word that is translated "pure" means "all," "whole," or "every." He was saying their joy should be the real thing. It didn't have to be faked or trumped-up. They were not obligated to give the "correct" appearance. Their joy could be genuine, even in the most difficult of circumstances.

Testing Has a Purpose (vv. 3-8): There is an indispensable quality in Christian living called "perseverance." James tells us that trials will come; they are unavoidable. When they do, the one who believes in Jesus Christ can experience genuine joy. There are reasons why joy can bubble up on top of our difficulties: because God is in the business of redemption, because God has promised to work for our good even in the most awful of situations, and because the testing of our faith develops perseverance.

James said, "The testing of your faith develops perseverance. Perseverance must finish its work so that you may be mature and complete, not lacking anything" (vv. 3-4). The Greek word translated "perseverance" here means "to bear up under." In the context of James 1:3-4, it means the ability to "bear courageously," "patiently endure," "hold steady with a good spirit," or "remain constant in spite of opposition or discouragement." The KJV calls it "patience." The NASB identifies it as "endurance." In the RSV, it is "steadfastness." The NEB labels it "fortitude." However it is translated into English, the word means that we learn to be steady when the pressure is on.

God uses the pressures and challenges of our lives to develop character, yet He has given us an assurance. "God is faithful; he will not let you be tempted beyond what you can bear. But when you are tempted, he will also provide a way out so that you can stand up under it" (1 Corinthians 10:13).

God understands that obstacles and pressures lie ahead in our Christian lives. We need to understand that He will go with us through those rough times rather than making them all disappear magically. That is why He calls us to learn perseverance.

Reversals Will Come (vv. 9-11): The new perspective of the believer keeps possessions and wealth in their proper place. Trials are part of the fabric of life, and reversals come to everyone.

James observed that a believer in the most lowly of circumstances is known and highly regarded by God himself.

Rather than being distressed about living in poverty, the person of limited means who has become a new person in Christ should have a new self-image—as a person of great worth in God's eyes.

James also observed that the believer who possesses great wealth has a new orientation regarding material possessions. The things of this world that make a person wealthy are always in jeopardy, while the things of true worth are spiritual and cannot be destroyed.

Love Stands the Test (v. 12): True happiness belongs to those who persevere when tested. Love is the motivation for not giving up in the struggle. James declared that the reward for enduring when tested is the crown of life. This is echoed in Revelation. "Be faithful, even to the point of death, and I will give you the crown of life" (2:10).

Faith Resists Temptation

James shifted his focus from "trials" to "temptations." He had insisted that trials are to be endured. Not so with temptations; they are to be resisted.

Temptation Is Bait (vv. 13-14): The experience of faith in Christ is nothing less than a new orientation for every area of life. A person of faith has a new sense of responsibility. It is inconsistent with this new life for the believer to play "the blame game" when faced with temptation. And it is especially abhorrent to blame God, because He is holy.

Unfortunately, people have a bad track record when it comes to taking responsibility. Even believers have been guilty of blaming God.

The Israelites played "the blame game" when the time came for them to enter the Promised Land. They had firsthand reports that the new land was a choice spot that produced food in abundance, but they were afraid of the people who lived there. Their fear caused them to rebel against God's clear direction. They began to grumble and complain.

In effect, they said, "We should have died in Egypt or in the desert. We should choose new leaders. Why is the Lord bringing us to this place so that we can fall by the sword?"

They blamed their leaders, in spite of their record of successes. They talked about replacing Moses and Aaron. And before the crisis ended, they threatened to kill them.

They finally blamed God, in spite of all the miracles He had performed to bring them to that place. God responded by postponing their possession of the Promised Land for 40 years, until that generation of grumblers had died.

It is a common error to make excuses by blaming someone else, even by blaming God. However, playing "the blame game" accomplishes nothing—at least nothing worthwhile. James was careful to point out that God should never be blamed, because "God cannot be tempted by evil, nor does he tempt anyone" (1:13).

When Jesus taught His disciples the prayer we call "The Lord's Prayer," He included this petition: "And lead us not into temptation" (Luke 11:4). Jesus was not suggesting that God would ever cause anyone to be tempted. He could never do that. It would be impossible, because God is holy. He does allow the faithful to experience trials, because they test and refine faith, but God has no part in temptation. In fact, the reference to temptation in the Lord's Prayer is a petition that God would have such control over our lives that He would keep us from being exposed to temptation's lure. When Jesus was in the Garden of Gethsemane, He instructed His disciples to pray that they would not fall into temptation (see Luke 22:40). Temptation is to be resisted.

James carefully observed that temptation does not come from an external source. It comes from within, from a person's own sinful nature, "Each one is tempted when, by his own evil desire, he is dragged away and enticed" (v. 14). Temptation is bait! It involves luring with the purpose of snaring.

We Are the Intended Victims (v. 15): The process of yielding to temptation can be traced in four simple steps:

Step One: Temptation begins when we allow our own evil desires to occupy our attention. This is the best place to defeat temptation—at the source. We can overcome temptation by walking in the Spirit while keeping our eyes focused on Christ.

Step Two: Once it has our attention, we are lured or baited by it, and entrapped.

Step Three: Then desire gives birth to sin. Just as focusing on Christ leads away from evil toward good, focusing on evil desire leads to the act of sin.

Step Four: Once sin becomes full-grown, it brings death.

Temptation in itself is not sin. Still, if we focus our attention on the temptation, we can be entrapped by sin. And the pay off for sin is always death—maybe not our immediate physical death, but surely another erosion of our spiritual health leading to eventual spiritual and/or physical death. When temptation confronts us, we should remember that its ultimate purpose is to bring about our spiritual demise.

Faith Accepts God's Enabling Gift

James began this section with a warning, "Don't be deceived" (v. 16). This phrase ties the warning to the previous words about temptation. He is saying, "Don't be deceived *about temptation*."

It is important that what James had to say about temptation does not end with the negative message of verse 15. How hopeless we would be if we were told only that temptation can lead to sin and death. Instead, in verses 17 and 18, James gave God's remedy for temptation, sin, and death. We are told that God, who gives good gifts, will counter the lure of temptation and overcome our bent toward sin.

God is the giver of everything that is good. He could not and would not bring anything into our lives for an evil purpose. In fact, His "good and perfect" gifts include "the word of truth" that made it possible for us to experience a spiritual new birth.

Why did God give us the word of truth? Why did He allow us to experience the new birth? James gave the answer, "That we might be a kind of firstfruits of all he created" (1:18).

In the Old Testament, the term "firstfruits" was used to refer to part of the harvest of agriculture. The "firstfruits" sometimes referred to the earliest; at other times, it meant choicest or best. Yet in both instances, it was considered holy to the Lord. When James referred to us as "firstfruits," he was saying that God wants to enable us to give our lives to Him as a choice sacrifice, as holy to the Lord. We could not do this in our own strength. Nevertheless, Jesus Christ makes it possible. In the letter to the Hebrews, we are told:

Since we have a great high priest who has gone through the heavens, Jesus the Son of God, let us hold firmly to the faith we profess. For we do not have a high priest who is unable to sympathize with our weaknesses, but we have one who has been tempted in every way, just as we are—yet was without sin. Let us then approach the throne of grace with confidence, so that we may receive mercy and find grace to help us in our time of need (4:14-16).

No one lives long without wondering why bad things happen. Many of us have repeatedly proven Murphy's Law: If anything can go wrong, it will. Bad things happen, and we are tested and tried when we face them. However sheltered we may be, we can't escape the whiplash of misfortune. We easily wonder how a good God allows so much evil to flourish; how a good world became so soiled with sin; how people, designed to be good, so routinely fail to be.

God allows us to go through tests, just like caring teachers and coaches test their students to help them. Those tests produce discipline, develop character, and enable us to become all we are meant to be. Certainly they do discomfort us. But God redeems our difficulties by using them for our good.

However, James made it clear that God would never tempt anyone. It is when we recognize the source of temptation that we can resist it. It is when we know the Source of our strength that we can find the help we need to overcome.

Tests and trials will come, but they should challenge us to deeper discipleship.

THE DIFFICULT PASSAGE:

Therefore, my brothers, be all the more eager to make your calling and election sure. For if you do these things, you will never fall (2 Peter 1:10).

BACKGROUND SCRIPTURE: 2 Peter 1:1-11

TRUTH TO REMEMBER:

We are called not only to be hearers of the Word but doers of the Word.

GUIDANCE ALONG OUR JOURNEY:

The scriptural background for this chapter is 2 Peter 1:1-11. Peter's second letter was a companion to 1 Peter, sent to the same audience. Peter's first letter was sent to encourage Christians who were being persecuted. It was circulated among the churches in Asia Minor, probably during Nero's persecution of the Church after the burning of Rome in A.D. 64. This second letter from Peter was written shortly before his death, somewhere between A.D. 65-67. In it, Peter specifically confronts false teachings regarding the Lord, the final coming of God, and self-indulgent freedom.

The difficult passage for this chapter deals with the believer's role in the work of salvation. Peter encourages believers "to be eager to make your calling and election sure" (1:10). This is similar to Paul's admonition, "Continue to work out your salvation with fear and trembling" (Philippians 2:12). We know that salvation is God's work; it is a matter of God's grace. However, just as it is begun by our participation in faith, it continues by our participation in faithfulness.

Because God in His sovereignty grants humans the freedom to make choices, we always have the possibility of choosing to turn from God. The churches to whom Peter wrote were full of people who exercised that very freedom by choosing to ignore or contradict the teachings and practices of the Church. However, most chose to glorify God by shaping their beliefs and practices according to the gospel. Today, Christians have the same freedom to make their own choices. Peter's shepherdlike concerns are appropriate for today's Church. May we heed his warnings and choose to grow in our faith in Christ Jesus.

Chapter 10

MAKE YOUR CALLING AND ELECTION SURE

THIS MAN CALLED Peter had been following the way of Christ for about 40 years. The Lord had brought him through some tough scrapes—but not this one. Peter knew that his time was short. It is generally believed that he was writing this letter from prison in Rome, just before his death. He had important things to say to the Church before he died. Perhaps he wondered how he should identify himself so that his words would be taken to heart. "Simon, the big fisherman"? "Simon, spokesman for the Twelve"? "Peter, disciple of Christ"? "Simon, the former denier"? "Simon Peter, sheep-feeder"?

After years of walking faithfully with the Lord, this good man opened his last letter to the Church with these words: "Simon Peter, a servant and apostle of Jesus Christ" (v. 1).

The grace of God had transformed a loudmouthed fisherman into an apostle of Christ. Peter called himself "apostle," and the words of this letter take on great authority. Also, he called himself a "servant," and his words take on the Spirit of Christ.

Our Lord Gives Us Everything We Need

This letter is a follow-up to a letter Peter had previously sent to the same readers (see 3:1). The purpose of the former letter had been to encourage believers to persevere in a time of suffering and persecution. This second letter was written to warn them against false teachers. However, Peter did not

open his letter with words of warning. He began with a reminder that God has given us everything that we need to live
a godly life. This was not written in the future tense. God
makes these resources available to us now.

The false teachers who had infiltrated the ranks of the
Church were teaching a heresy that has come to be known as
Gnosticism. It took many different forms. The name Gnosticism comes from the Greek word *gnosis*; it means knowledge.
They claimed that they were among those to whom a secret
knowledge had been revealed. This special knowledge was
considered superior to faith. It was revealed only to an elite
number, because they believed that the ordinary masses could
never understand it.

Gnostics taught that the creation of this world was a mis-
take, the work of a foolish creator without the permission of
God. They maintained that all material things were evil.
Therefore, God is forever separate from this world. However,
God devised a plan to enable the Gnostics (the "knowers") to
receive a special revelation, making it possible for them to return to the spiritual realm and be reunited with Him.

Gnostic thought was at odds with almost every cardinal
Christian doctrine: (1) Forget about salvation by grace
through faith. Salvation is for the spiritually elite who possess
secret knowledge. (2) Away with the incarnation of Christ.
God could not actually become a man since all matter is evil.
(3) Out goes the hope of redemption from sin by Christ on
the Cross. Redemption is simply the release of our imprisoned
spirits from these sinful bodies. (4) Down with holy living. It
is either impossible because there is evil in everything, or the
prevalence of evil in everything makes it necessary to live as
an ascetic, completely apart from the world.

Today's New Age religions closely resemble ancient Gnostic cults, especially in their notion that all of us are one with
God and that self-awareness and self-realization (which is the
same as God-consciousness) will bring us bliss. If we are all in
our inner essence one with God, there is no need to know

anything other than one's self. Historical revelation, other than offering helpful advice, has little value. Nor does Christ fill any ultimate end, for He is reduced to nothing more than an enlightened teacher. For them, Jesus is not the God-Man who entered our world to save us from sin. He was merely a self-actualized man with whom we can identify as our elder brother. The divine powers He drew upon are open channels that we can draw upon too.

Whether ancient or modern, Gnostics refuse to live by faith and demand personal, firsthand knowledge. Thus in our time, New Age books and human-potential seminars, hypnotic televangelists, and Asian mystics all attract devotees. All promise special insights, supernatural revelations, and altered states of consciousness. A privileged knowledge derived from personal, immediate, firsthand encounters with some "higher power" becomes the goal.

How can we know that we have not been led astray? What is the proper measure of the message of truth? How are we to respond to false teachers and false teachings?

Know Christ Personally: It all centers on Christ. What is the proper measure of the truth? It is Christ, the Truth. How can we keep from being led astray? Know Christ personally. How should we respond to false teachers and false teachings? Give a living witness to the presence of the crucified Christ.

The false teachers were saying that those who possessed secret knowledge would come to experience union with God. Peter established common ground by beginning with a point of agreement. He agreed that knowledge is important, but the kind that is most important is knowledge of Christ.

When Paul wrote to the Colossians about the problem of Gnosticism, he echoed Peter's response about the importance of being centered on Christ. "See to it that no one takes you captive through hollow and deceptive philosophy, which depends on human tradition and the basic principles of this world rather than on Christ" (Colossians 2:8).

In this letter, Peter tells us:

- We can have grace and peace in abundance "through the knowledge of God and of Jesus our Lord" (1:2).
- "Through our knowledge of [Christ]," we have everything we need for godly living (1:3).
- If Christlike virtues are exercised, the knowledge of our Lord Jesus Christ will be fruitful (1:8).

In each of these three verses, the word Peter uses for knowledge in reference to Christ is *epignosis*, which means "increasing knowledge." It is knowledge which is moving in the direction of the thing that it seeks to know. This is not just head knowledge; it is personal experience. Peter is speaking of knowing Christ better and better, of having an ever-deepening relationship with Him personally.

When we are on intimate terms with Jesus, He gives us everything we need for godly living. In Paul's letter to the Colossians, he said, "Your own completeness is only realized in him, who is the ruler over all authorities, and the supreme power over all powers" (Colossians 2:10, PHILLIPS). The power that makes our faithfulness possible is not our own. It is the divine power of Jesus within us.

Appropriate His Promises: Peter tells us that everything we need for godly living is available to us "through our knowledge of [Christ]" (v. 3) and "his very great and precious promises" (v. 4).

Christ has become the guarantor of all the promises of God. Paul put it this way in his letter to the Corinthians: "For no matter how many promises God has made, they are 'Yes' in Christ" (2 Corinthians 1:20).

Receive His Spirit: When Peter says that we can "participate in the divine nature" (v. 4), his language sounds strangely like that of the false teachers. However, Peter was not talking about our spirits being absorbed into the deity; he was speaking of union with Christ in this world. For Peter, participation in the divine nature is not the *final goal* of the believer but the *starting point*. That is what Jesus meant when He said, "You will receive power when the Holy Spirit comes on you"

(Acts 1:8). Paul spoke of the same thing when he referred to the "mystery, which is Christ in you, the hope of glory" (Colossians 1:27).

And He Keeps on Giving

Vital Christian living is a cooperative venture between God and an individual. Peter said the believer is to "make every effort" (v. 5) to live by faith. This sounds a bit like Paul's advice to the Philippians: "Continue to work out your salvation with fear and trembling, for it is God who works in you to will and to act according to his good purpose" (2:12-13). Even our ability to cooperate with God is a gift of His grace! God is always giving all that we need—and more.

The word in verse 5 that is translated "add" actually means "to generously provide at one's own expense." The word originated in the Greek drama festivals. There were very wealthy individuals who helped to finance the production of plays, often at great expense. This word became an expression of their generous and costly cooperation. When Peter used the term in verse 5, he meant more than "add these things to your faith." He was actually saying, "Lavishly equip your faith with these things."

Faith: It is saving faith that brings us into a relationship with God. Yet, that faith only marks the beginning of our relationship with Him. Peter tells us that a believer should take personal initiative in building on that faith. Even though human effort is inadequate for the task, it is absolutely essential. We are to use every bit of determination that we have to cooperate with what God is doing.

Goodness: An essential quality in the exercise of faith is goodness or virtue. Peter had already used this word as a characteristic of Jesus (v. 3). It has to do with moral excellence. This same Christlike quality is to become evident in the character of the believer.

Knowledge: Knowledge of God and His will are necessary

for faith to produce obedience to God. False teachers claimed to have superior knowledge that was not available to the masses, special knowledge that came as a result of illumination and was beyond reason or faith. Peter sets things straight. Knowledge is actually experienced within the context of faith and virtue, and it is progressively acquired. This knowledge is not reserved for an elite few; it is for all those who have faith in Christ Jesus.

Self-control: Some of the false teachers insisted that their superior knowledge had released them from the need for self-control. Peter countered them with the truth that true knowledge leads to self-control. Paul gave self-control as one aspect of the fruit of the Spirit (Galatians 5:23). Only when life is under the Spirit's control can we demonstrate self-control.

Perseverance: Self-control produces perseverance, the ability to remain steady when under pressure. Perseverance is faith overcoming difficulties. It does not merely outlast the opposition. It courageously endures because of the joy that is yet to come (see Hebrews 12:2).

Godliness: Perseverance produces godliness, which is both a reverence for God and a respect for other people. Godliness cannot be falsified. It comes from being alive to God and possessed by His Spirit. As a believer's life comes increasingly under His control, the likeness of Christ is more fully reflected.

Brotherly Kindness: The Greek word is *philadelphia*. It identifies the family affection that exists among believers. Within the Church, we regard one another as children of the same Father.

Love: Here Peter spoke of *agape* love. This is a love like the love of God. When we "participate in the divine nature," surely we will reflect the very quality of God's love. Christian faith is the soil from which all of these qualities grow. And love encompasses all of them.

Believers who cultivate these Christian qualities will experience spiritual growth. However, those who ignore these virtues and do not make the effort to add to their faith take the risk of becoming "nearsighted and blind" (v. 9). When Peter talks about falling in verse 10, it is understood that it is the nearsighted and blind who are prone to stumble and fall. The sad truth is that those who become spiritually blind will not attain the promise of life eternal. When Peter says that we are to "possess these qualities in increasing measure" (v. 8), we are reminded that a Christian life that is not moving ahead is falling behind. There is no plateau in the course of Christian maturity.

Give God Everything You Have

Peter encourages believers to exert themselves in order to make their calling and election sure. The concepts of "calling" and "election" would be very confusing if it were not for the fact that Jesus explained it very clearly. On the night in the Upper Room, as Jesus was preparing His disciples for all that lay ahead, He said to them, "You did not choose me, but I chose you and appointed you to go and bear fruit" (John 15:16).

Christ calls and chooses. God has clearly taken the initiative in His relationship with us. It has always been our privilege to respond to God's initiating grace. The fact that He calls us and chooses us does not change the fact that we choose how we will respond to Him.

That night in the Upper Room, Jesus also said, "If you obey my commands, you will remain in my love, just as I have obeyed my Father's commands and remain in his love" (15:10). He calls and chooses us, and we choose how we will respond.

The way that Peter used the expression "calling and election" actually refers to everything that is involved in Christ's invitation to repent, to be saved, and to serve Him. Yet, Peter was very careful to remind them—and us—that while God has given everything that is needed for godly living, He still requires our effort.

Faith is always a response to God's activity. Initially, faith is an affirming "yes" to God's invitation to enter into a saving relationship with Him. However, faith does not stop there, for God's grace does not stop there. God continues to be merciful, and He empowers believers to respond by growing and maturing in their faith.

It is our earnestness in allowing God's Spirit to have control of our lives that makes our calling and election certain. Yes, God calls. Yes, God chooses us. However, His invitation and choice await our response—our response that says, "Yes, I will receive the gift of salvation. Yes, I will allow the Holy Spirit to control my life. Yes, I will make every effort to equip my faith with the things of God."

Verse 5 has a striking similarity with what Peter had to say in verse 10: "Make every effort to add to your faith" (v. 5). "Be all the more eager to make your calling and election sure" (v. 10). He made this emphasis again at the close of the letter: "Make every effort to be found spotless, blameless and at peace with him" (3:14).

It is left to us to choose what our relationship to God will be. That relationship is developed through a lifelong process. In this passage of Scripture, we see Peter at the end of that process. Peter referred to himself as "a servant of Jesus Christ" (v. 1). The word Peter used is *doulos,* which actually means more than servant; it means "slave." After walking with Jesus for about four decades, Peter had established a warm and wonderful relationship with our Lord. He celebrated the fact that he had become a slave.

As a slave of Jesus Christ, Peter's life was not his own. He was owned by Christ. He was Christ's possession. As a slave of Jesus Christ, Peter owed loyalty and obedience to the Master. As a slave, Peter's whole life was at the disposal of Christ, his Owner. He was always in Christ's service. There was no time when he was on his own.

Peter's own life as a slave of Jesus Christ is a perfect illustration of what God wants from each of us. We are called to give ourselves to Him completely.

Conclusion

God has given us everything that we need for godly living. Because of His great love, He keeps on giving goodness, knowledge, self-control, perseverance, godliness, brotherly kindness, and love in increasing measure as we ask Him.

How should we respond to One who gives us everything that we need and more? After all that He has done, after all that He has given, what should we do?

We should give Him ourselves completely! That is how we "make our calling and election sure." That is how we "do [all] these things." That is what it means to have Jesus Christ as Lord and Savior.

THE DIFFICULT WORDS:

Hand this man over to Satan, so that the sinful nature may be destroyed and his spirit saved on the day of the Lord (1 Corinthians 5:5).

BACKGROUND SCRIPTURE: 1 Corinthians 5:1-13

TRUTH TO REMEMBER:

In a world that has become polluted by sin, the believer's life is to reflect both the purity of the Church and the redemptive power of Christ.

GUIDANCE ALONG OUR JOURNEY:

The problem that Paul addresses in the **BACKGROUND SCRIPTURE** for this chapter is incest. We understand Paul's abhorrence regarding this particular sin, especially the flaunting of an incestuous relationship by someone in the church. However, what is bothersome about this passage to most people today is the way Paul dealt with the offender. He didn't use the word "excommunication," but that aptly describes Paul's verdict. Four times in this short chapter, Paul told the Corinthians to put this immoral man out of the church. He wrote, "With such a man do not even eat" (v. 11).

The idea of putting someone out of the church doesn't sit well with most of us. That sort of action is out of step with our desire to keep the peace. We have the idea that if we overlook wrongdoing, we can keep the offender in the church where there is help. Yet, does it really help people if we ignore the presence of evil in their lives? Or by overlooking the problem, do we actually enable them to continue their wrong conduct?

Paul's message to the Corinthians—and to us—is that the Church must not have a lax or complacent attitude about evil practices in the Church. He warns that there is great danger for the Church and the individual when evil is condoned among believers. This chapter provides a reminder that Christ's Body is to be kept pure. And it shows that He always seeks to be redemptive.

Chapter 11

HAND THAT ONE OVER TO SATAN!

THERE WAS TROUBLE in the church at Corinth! The credibility of Jesus' followers was being tarnished by sexual immorality between a man in the church and his "father's wife" (v. 1) Paul referred to the sin of incest by using the same language as the Old Testament law: "Do not have sexual relations with your *father's wife*" (Leviticus 18:8, emphasis added). Incest was not only a violation of Jewish law, it was considered so vile that even the pagan Greco-Roman culture condemned it.

Informed of this relationship, Paul reacted! He didn't assure everyone involved that God loves them and accepts them right where they are. He called it what it was, "immorality" (v. 1).

In sobering ways, the sexual standards of contemporary society closely resemble those of ancient Corinth. One of the leaders of the "sexual revolution," Helen Gurley Brown (for years the editor of *Cosmopolitan*), once proposed a new definition for promiscuity. She suggested that to be promiscuous is to have sex with more than one person on a given day. So long as you limit yourself on a daily basis to one person, supposedly you are OK. (Does monogamy only last 24 hours?)

Paul, writing to the folks in Corinth, vented his moral outrage, his shock at such immorality. He didn't hesitate when he learned what was happening. He reacted, and he sharply condemned it.

Today, we see little outrage, little condemnation of evil,

for we've slowly grown accustomed to television programs and movies which glorify all sorts of sexuality. In many circles today, being unfaithful to one's spouse hardly raises eyebrows. Pornography is no longer strictly banned in most communities. "Family," long understood to mean a union of man and woman with their children, has been redefined in our society as any group of people who enjoy living together. Anything goes. Few dare to stand up and say "no" to anything.

In this passage, Paul objected to the permissiveness displayed by the people in the church at Corinth. They seemed unwilling to confront the evildoers. Rather than embarrass anyone, they chose to ignore the problem. They seem to have confused *love* with *approval*. Loving sinners seemed to mean overlooking their behavior.

Paul's words stand in sharp contrast to this. Paul judged and condemned immorality, and he commanded believers to shape up. Paul said plainly that flagrant immoral behavior cannot be tolerated in the Church. However, Paul's directive to the Corinthians is shocking. "Hand this man over to Satan" (v. 5). This is the apostle who would write so powerfully about love later in this same letter (chap. 13). How could he urge that church to hand a man over to Satan?

This Saying Is Hard to Understand

Paul used this same terminology about handing someone over to Satan in 1 Timothy 1:20. Apparently, it was an expression Paul routinely used for expelling someone from the Church. In Paul's thinking, to be outside the fellowship of the Church is to be in the sphere of Satan, where evil principalities and powers are at work in people's lives to destroy them. For Paul, it wasn't a matter of removing this man from the ranks of the Christians and placing him in the ranks of the world, because this man had already made that choice himself, within his own heart.

There have been those who suggest that Paul intended

that the man should die when he said, "Hand this man over to Satan, so that the sinful nature may be destroyed" (v. 5). Nothing could be farther from the truth! This is the same kind of language Paul used in Galatians 5:24. "Those who belong to Christ Jesus have crucified the sinful nature with its passions and desires." Paul stated his concern for this man that "his spirit [may be] saved on the day of the Lord" (v. 5). It was Paul's hope that this man's sinful nature would be crucified with Christ so that he might be saved.

We must acknowledge that we don't know very much about this situation. Paul was careful not to reveal anything more than the barest details, but he was obviously aware of them. Otherwise, it is unlikely that he could have "already passed judgment" (v. 3) on the church member involved. However, it will be helpful to list the harsh realities of 1 Corinthians 5 that we do know:

- A man in the church was involved in a flagrant incestuous relationship. It could not escape notice and should not be condoned, yet it was.
- This problem had already been dealt with in a previous letter to the Corinthians that we do not have (see v. 9).
- The man involved in this relationship had no intention of changing, and the church had ignored Paul's advice.
- In the present letter, Paul stated his judgment about the matter. He told them four times in this short chapter that they should expel the evildoer.
- The Corinthian Christians were proud of their open-mindedness about this man's sin. Paul told them that they should be grieving instead.
- By their permissiveness, the Corinthians were sending the wrong message to the world.
- Paul told them what they were to do next—handle the matter in a meeting of the whole church. Apparently, since it was known by all and had contaminated the whole church, it was to be dealt with by the whole group in a spirit of unity and agreement.

- Paul was specific about how it was to be done—dealt with in an atmosphere where Christ's presence was powerfully felt, with the hope that the man might choose to repent.
- Paul told the Corinthians to take care of this problem before the whole church became corrupted. He compared sin in that church to yeast in a lump of dough. A very small amount of yeast can go through all of the dough and change it.
- Through all of this, the concern was the redemption of the man and the purity of the church at Corinth.

This Saying Is Even Harder to Put into Practice

None of us really wants to be part of a church that is judgmental and small-spirited. We loathe the idea of trading the warm spirit of the Body of Christ for the harsh specter of an inquisition. We can hardly imagine excommunicating anyone. And Paul would be the first to say, "Amen."

Neither Paul nor the Corinthians wanted the church to become judgmental or harsh in dealing with people. Yet in chapter 5, we find them in the last stages of very serious conflict resolution. Although we don't have an overview of how this problem was dealt with up to this point, Paul was very specific about how they were to proceed—our Lord's way.

The whole process for handling such problems has been clearly outlined by Jesus, and it is important for us to know and follow the steps He prescribed in Matthew 18.

Step 1: *Go and talk with him or her.* "If your brother sins against you, go and show him his fault, just between the two of you. If he listens to you, you have won your brother over" (v. 15).

Step 2: *Go again, with others.* "But if he will not listen, take one or two others along, so that 'every matter may be established by the testimony of two or three witnesses'" (v. 16).

Step 3: *Take it to the church.* "If he refuses to listen to them, tell it to the church" (v. 17).

Step 4: *Expel the evildoer.* "And if he refuses to listen even to the church, treat him as you would a pagan or a tax collector" (v. 17).

Guidelines for Our Lord's Way

From Paul's handling of this negative situation in Corinth, some positive principles emerge. When we deal with difficult circumstances within the church, we should observe these same guidelines:

Appropriateness: The situation in Corinth was very serious. It had to be dealt with for the sake of the individual and for the reputation and purity of the church. The process was appropriate for the serious circumstances. That is not always the case. There are times when what may be gained by this whole process is not worth the cost. Not every misunderstanding or annoyance deserves this kind of intense scrutiny. And there are circumstances when it is best to forget what has happened and move on. The question of appropriateness must always be considered before embarking on this trail.

Confidentiality: In order to deal with this scandalous situation, Paul had to be fully informed of the details. Still, he was able to announce his verdict to the whole congregation without giving any personal information about the individuals involved. He did not betray in any way what was entrusted to him. Great harm is done by individuals who talk too much. It is as important to keep a trust by remaining silent as it is to speak the truth in love. And in the Church, there are no Lone Rangers and no vigilantes.

Divine Guidance: Paul was very specific about how this matter of expelling the immoral brother was to be handled by the church:

- They were to assemble in the Lord's name (v. 4).
- They were to remember that Paul was with them in spir-

it (v. 4). In other words, they are doing this with proper authority.

- They were to be certain that the power of the Lord Jesus was present (v. 4).
- While they were enjoying the beauty of the Lord's presence, they were to sever ties with the one who was unrepentant (v. 5). They were not only following the Lord's procedure; they were seeking His will and following His guidance.

Redemption: The true goal of this entire process was not the permanent expulsion of the immoral believer, but repentance. From the very beginning, that should have been the prayer of everyone involved. These measures had to be taken with the hope that they would stir the brother to renew his commitment to Christ. Even if the immoral brother would not repent, their aim was not punitive, but remedial and redemptive.

Conclusion

Sociologist Marsha G. Witten, after studying the sermons preached in typical Protestant churches, wrote a book entitled *All Is Forgiven: The Secular Message in American Protestantism.* She found, with few exceptions, that God no longer appears as a high and holy "wholly other." The holy Yahweh of Mount Sinai seems to have disappeared, along with His law. Instead, He's described as a tender-hearted "Daddy, Sufferer, Lover." He is generally "portrayed exclusively or predominantly in terms of the positive functions He serves for men and women. Chief among these functions is one that can be labeled 'therapeutic.'" God loves us "regardless of merit in the same way—freely and equally." He never judges, never condemns, never commands.

How out of character with God's Word is this picture of God! This is not the view of God we see in Paul's handling of sin in the Corinthian church.

Common wisdom says that one bad apple can ruin the whole bunch. That is why grocery shoppers examine bags of apples—or pints of strawberries, for that matter—very closely. They want to make sure that they do not purchase a bag of apples with a bad one in it. Should Christ expect any less of His church?

THE DIFFICULT WORDS:

Do not be yoked together with unbelievers. For what do righteousness and wickedness have in common? Or what fellowship can light have with darkness? (2 Corinthians 6:14).

BACKGROUND SCRIPTURE: 1 Corinthians 6:12-20; 2 Corinthians 6:14 —7:1

TRUTH TO REMEMBER:

Holy living is dependent on the believer's willingness to reject the idolatry and immorality of the culture in which he or she lives.

GUIDANCE ALONG OUR JOURNEY:

Every new believer soon finds out that it takes real effort to live a Christian life in an unchristian world. It cannot be lived by hiding in the sanctuary any more than it can be accomplished by becoming immersed in the things of the world.

Paul expressed his concern by saying, "Do not be yoked together with unbelievers" (2 Corinthians 6:14).

Paul also knew it is impossible to live rightly as believers without having ties with unbelievers. In fact, Christians are called by Christ to go into the world and make disciples. We cannot accomplish this mission without having meaningful ties with people in the world. However, Paul was concerned for believers who formed their closest attachments with non-Christians, because the life values and goals are so different.

Christians live with this tension daily. It is unavoidable. This conflict will be either dynamic or destructive. While improper relationships can compromise Christian standards and jeopardize an effective witness, Spirit-led relationships can lead to salvation and spiritual growth. The issue is who is going to influence whom.

YOKED WITH UNBELIEVERS

MOST OF US KNOW very little about horses. Even fewer are familiar with work horses other than the matched eight-horse hitch of Clydesdales seen in commercials. Except among the Amish and a few others, field work in North America has been mechanized for a long, long time.

Only the oldest among us can remember working a field with a team of horses. Some of us can vaguely recall stories our parents told of their early days on the farm, where horses were indispensable. So, except for parades and fall hayrides, we don't see a team of horses very often and certainly most would not know how to harness them. The terms "gee" and "haw" are seldom used today, and the difference between the lead horse and the off horse are concepts largely unknown. We have instrument panels in the dashboards of our cars but can't fathom what the farmer meant when he said, "If horses were perfect, we wouldn't need dashboards on buggies."

All that to say that we do not have the background of personal experience to readily understand what Paul meant when he said, "Do not be yoked together with unbelievers" (2 Corinthians 6:14). "Be ye not unequally yoked together with unbelievers" is the way the King James Version puts it, while the *New Revised Standard Version* translates it, "Do not be mismatched with unbelievers."

Modern paraphrases try to help us understand this passage by updating it. "Don't link up with unbelievers and try to work with them" (PHILLIPS). "Don't become partners with those who reject God" (TM). Still, none of the modern paraphrases have the power of the image of a poorly matched team struggling to work together.

We can visualize the portrait painted in Deuteronomy 22:10, however, where the Hebrews were commanded, "Do not plow with an ox and a donkey yoked together." This paints a ludicrous picture—a big ox and a little donkey harnessed together. The ox would not have been able to plow a straight furrow because of the contrary little animal alongside it. This seems to be the picture Paul is presenting here.

The apostle counsels, "Do not be yoked together with unbelievers." What did that mean then and what should it mean in our daily lives? That's our challenge. Let's see if we can find some answers.

First, Some Background

The apostle Paul didn't jump up from his nap one day and say to his secretary Timothy, "Hey, Tim, I just had an idea. Write this down. 'Do not be yoked together with unbelievers.' No, change that to, 'Don't be mismatched with unbelievers.'"

It all took place in the real world. A world where Paul clearly understood the sensual nature of a city like Corinth and was troubled by what was happening with the new Christians there.

Corinth was quite a place. It was situated on the isthmus that separated the Peloponnesian peninsula from mainland Greece. It was near two major ports: Cenchrea, which provided access to the Aegean Sea, and Lechaeum, on the Gulf of Corinth, an arm of the Ionian Sea. Small ships and/or cargo could be moved overland the few miles from one port to the other, bypassing the dangerous 200-mile trip south around the Cape of Maleae.

The Corinth of Paul's day had about 700,000 inhabitants and was noted for its wealth. The Corinthians were a sophisticated, cosmopolitan people. Since the culture revolved around money, the greatest divisions were economic rather than racial. It was a wide-open city with many opportunities for idle sailors or financially-secure citizens to spend their money on sensual pleasures. All of this was overshadowed by the worship of the cult of Aphrodite, with its focus on the use of prostitutes as part of worship.

Into that wealthy, sinful, and corrupt city, Paul came preaching about One who called for purity and servanthood. This new belief system promised great rewards, but it also made significant demands. It called for a complete break with all that was traditional, the so-called "sacred" of the day, and the sometimes enjoyable.

However, we've only been looking at the surface. What's at issue is far more fundamental—a matter of loyalty to God or the gods. And the upsetting question as to whether and how much it matters.

A Collision of Gods

Or to put it more correctly, a collision between God and the local gods. Corinth's colorful history provided a broad menu of gods to worship.

Corinth began as a Greek city. Much later in its history it was conquered by the Romans. In 44 B.C., Julius Caesar founded a Roman colony, composed in large part of freed slaves. Many first-century slaves were highly skilled; they often had more education and training than their owners. These former slaves were not Romans. They came from Greece, Syria, Judea, and Egypt and brought all their customs and all their gods with them. These were mixed with the local gods and customs.

Our temptation is to focus solely on the worship of the goddess Aphrodite. However, Paul's message goes far beyond contrasting between the immorality of worship in the pagan temple and the purity expected of those who followed Jesus.

Those who converted to Christianity in Corinth often came out of pagan cults where many gods were worshiped.

None of their old gods required exclusive devotion. And it was not uncommon for new Christians to claim their devotion to Christ while continuing to have some allegiance to their old gods. Certainly this was not acceptable, but it is an indication of both the difficulty and the necessity of making a break with the pagan world. These cults had such a pervasive influence on daily life that it was difficult for Christians to function without giving the impression that they were involved in pagan idolatry. It was difficult to shop in the marketplace because much of the food that was sold there had been sacrificed to idols. It was a problem to eat at a public gathering or at the home of an old friend because they would serve sacrificial food. Public gatherings were frequently held in the pagan temples, and believers feared that their presence would indicate that they approved of the heathen rituals that were performed there.

In many Roman cities, local temples also served as centers for civic life. Some temples had stadiums built adjacently, and there were close ties between the athletic and theatric events held in the stadium and religious observances. Other temples served as the meeting place for public officers and assemblies. Many temples had adjacent facilities for cooking and banquet halls. The banquet halls were more than simply places to eat, like contemporary restaurants. Because of their close association with the temple deity, the meals served there were understood to have some religious significance. The meat probably came from temple sacrifices; priests and priestesses presided over the meals. People attended the banquet halls with the hope of the god's blessing on their business deals or political alliances.

Separation from the world was a difficult thing in Corinth. In truth, it is an ongoing struggle for every generation. How should believers associate with those who are outside of the Christian fellowship? Absolute separation is clearly impossible and not desirable. On the other hand, unrestricted participation in the world would be ruinous. Paul's warning makes sense. Don't be harnessed with unbelievers. Don't compromise the integrity of your faith. Don't ever forget that you are to be one of God's holy people.

Paul asked, "What do righteousness and wickedness have in common? Or what fellowship can light have with darkness?" (v. 14). The answer is obvious. None! You can no more mix righteousness and wickedness than you can have light and darkness in the same spot at the same time.

Then Paul wanted to know, "What harmony is there between Christ and Belial?" (v. 15). "Belial," a word borrowed from the Hebrew language meaning "worthless," was used to identify Satan. The word "harmony" is the foundational word for our word "symphony." In the Greek translation of the Old Testament, the Septuagint, the same word in Daniel 3:5 is translated "bagpipe" by the NASB. Let the picture capture your imagination. Can you imagine the Lord and Satan marching side by side in a parade, playing the bagpipes? Or, can you imagine God and the devil invited to play in the same symphonic orchestra? Of course, not.

A fundamental issue here is the character of the god they choose to serve. Paul reminds the Corinthians that the God of the Bible is a jealous God, allowing no rivals. And that brings us to the practical side of Paul's word to the Corinthians.

A Collision of Cultures

An atheist in Corinth would have been lonely. Everyone was religious. The worship of the gods had so completely saturated the Corinthian culture that it was nearly impossible to find the line between the religious and the secular—if, indeed, there was one. That made it easy, and apparently attractive, for some Christians to continue to live like pagans. They could place the Christian God at the head of their list of gods and continue to live the way they had always lived. That resulted in no disruption of their social life or change in business practices.

However, God said, "Come out from them and be separate" (v. 17). These words were originally a call to the exiles in Babylon to leave their comfortable life and return to the challenges of rebuilding Jerusalem (see Isaiah 52:11). Here, Paul called for Christians to discontinue their close relationships with anyone involved in sinful activities, lest those alliances lead them into sin.

Those were tough words then. They are tough words now. Corinth, in some ways, reminds us of a middle-class or upper-middle-class suburb in any prosperous North American city. Neither churches nor church members have been immunized against the infectious nature of our culture any more than the Corinthians were. Today, Christians face the same temptations to compromise for social acceptance or financial advantage as the Corinthian Christians did.

Missionaries who return to North America after years of service abroad are often saddened by compromises they see when they tour churches. Occasionally, a courageous one will call the church away from its infatuation with the world to a new resolve to live for Jesus. Often, it's a call we have difficulty hearing. Yet, the Lord still says, "Come out from them and be separate."

"Therefore glorify God in your body" (1 Corinthians 6:20). The Corinthians lived at a time and in a place where what we used to call "the sins of the flesh" were common. Paul chose an example in 1 Corinthians to illustrate how Christians should and should not treat their bodies. He talked about prostitution, an activity that was acceptable to most Corinthians and considered an act of worship by many.

"A Christian should not buy the services of a prostitute." That was the meaning of Paul's forthright declaration, "Shall I . . . take the members of Christ and unite them with a prostitute? Never!" (v. 15). Tucked in behind Paul's argument was the radically different value Greek philosophers and Christian believers placed on the human body.

Some Corinthian converts engaged in relationships that

blurred the lines between themselves and their pagan neighbors. Going to temple banquet halls and visiting prostitutes were actions that were completely accepted in their society but which were contrary to wholehearted allegiance to Christ. These Corinthians were definitely *in* the world; however, their actions indicated that they were also *of* the world.

The Greeks said that the body and the spirit were separate. That led to one of two paths. Some Greeks did everything they could to destroy the desires of the body in order to shatter its influence over the spirit. The more common view was to conclude that since the body was of little value, you could do what you wanted with it. Eat what you want. Do what you please. It didn't make any difference, for only the spirit counted.

But Paul said, "Your body is a temple of the Holy Spirit, who is in you, whom you have from God. . . . You are not your own; you were bought at a price. Therefore glorify God with your body" (1 Corinthians 6:19-20). Since the body is a temple of the Most High God, it makes a big difference what Christians do with it.

Conclusion

A yoke was a simple apparatus used to bind and control "beasts of burden." It became a visual illustration of controlling powers, of ownership, and of service. A relationship between two parties was at times described in terms of a yoke.

In the Roman Empire, slaves were considered property. Tags of ownership in the form of earrings, chords, chains, or a brand were placed on slaves, thus indicating their status and to whom they belonged. These ownership tags came to be figuratively called yokes.

In Israelite tradition, the yoke eventually symbolized the covenant relationship between the people and the Lord. But, unlike the economic and political tags of slave-ownership, the covenant was a joy to bear. Jesus and the early Christian community spoke of the yoke as a symbol of the covenant be-tween himself and His followers. As such, it emphasized the subservient relationship between individuals and the Lord and the binding together of "yokefellows." This relationship is characterized by servant love, not by domination and disre-gard. No wonder Paul said, "Do not be yoked together with unbelievers," for such a combination could never truly reflect our relationship in Christ.

THE DIFFICULT WORDS:

If anyone does not provide for his relatives, and especially for his immediate family, he has denied the faith and is worse than an unbeliever (1 Timothy 5:8).

BACKGROUND SCRIPTURE: 1 Timothy 5:3-16

TRUTH TO REMEMBER:

Christians have clear responsibilities to fulfill their obligations of honor and love to their families.

GUIDANCE ALONG OUR JOURNEY:

God's basic expectations for His people are spelled out in the Ten Commandments. The first one, "You shall have no other gods before me" (Exodus 20:3), is the foundation for the second, third, and fourth. Together, they establish the basis for a relationship between God and human beings. The last six deal with God's expectations for people in their relationships with one another. The fifth commandment, "Honor your father and your mother" (20:12), is the foundation for all the remaining commandments, because it establishes the standard for the relationship between children and their parents. This becomes the starting point for society and the norm for all other relationships.

The family was God's idea, and behind the concept of "father" is the universal fatherhood of God. It was God who set in order the whole scheme of family relationships. When Paul told the Ephesians that he prayed for them, he said, "For this reason I kneel before the Father, from whom his whole family in heaven and on earth derives its name" (Ephesians 3:14). The concept of "family" is so basic to God's plan that it applies not only to the household, but to the Church and all humankind as well.

This chapter deals with a hard saying about family relationships within the home and within the Church. This is a relevant issue in a society that seems to be losing its bearings regarding the family. It will help us get back to the basics of familial responsibilities.

Chapter 13

WORSE THAN AN UNBELIEVER

HOW BAD DO YOU have to be to be worse than an unbeliever in our day? That depends. "I know people who never go to church, who are better than some so-called Christians I've met," a man said to me one day about a person in our congregation. My temptation was to give a flippant response, such as, "You're right, but you should have seen him before the Lord began to work on him."

But I didn't.

Fortunately, our world has people who, either by nature or training, live on a higher ethical and moral level than some who attend church regularly. There are people who testify to God's saving grace in their lives who continue to have difficulty with attractive temptations to return to their old life. Not all these people successfully combat those temptations.

On the other hand, some unbelievers have "the morals of an alley cat," to borrow a descriptive phrase.

How bad do you have to be to be worse than an unbeliever in our day? That all depends on which unbeliever we use for comparison. It also presumes that there are standards to measure conduct. That some actions are right and others wrong. That there is both good and bad, ethical and unethical behavior.

The whole question becomes more complicated if we equate any kind of personal action with salvation. Is there anything we can, or should, do to earn our salvation? Or to put it another way, do we receive the forgiveness of sins and the promise of eternal life with a loving God as the result of something we do or choose not to do? The New Testament answer is clear. "It is by grace you have been saved, through faith—and this not from yourselves, it is the gift of God" (Ephesians 2:8).

We are saved by grace and grace alone.

But you say, "We must have faith." And you are right.

However, faith does not save us. "By *grace* you have been saved . . . it is the gift of God." This foundational truth is affirmed in 2 Timothy in these words, "God . . . has saved us and called us to a holy life—not because of anything we have done but because of his own purpose and grace" (1:9).

What then did Paul mean when he said, "If anyone does not provide for his relatives, and especially for his immediate family, he has denied the faith and is worse than an unbeliever" (1 Timothy 5:8)? Was he suggesting a new means of salvation? Or did he have a different message? Let's explore those questions by first taking a look at Ephesus, the city where Timothy lived when Paul wrote to him, and then examining the challenge Christians faced there.

First-Century Ephesus

Ephesus was a great city. At least, Paul must have thought so. He spent more time there than at any other place during his missionary work. It was a city of wealth, power, and beautiful buildings. Among them was the temple dedicated to Artemis (whom the Romans called Diana). It is remembered as one of the "seven wonders of the ancient world," along with the pyramids of Egypt, the hanging gardens of Babylon, the massive statue of the Greek sun god Helios at the harbor at Rhodes, and other remarkable artistic and architectural achievements.

Located in modern Turkey, Ephesus is now a pile of rocky rubble, destroyed by major earthquakes in the fourth and seventh centuries and never rebuilt. By contrast, first-century

Ephesus was a regional center that exerted administrative control over more than 500 cities in the Roman province of Asia. It had about the same mixture of the sacred, sensual, and sinful you would have found in any major city in the first-century Roman world—if you added money.

Back then, Ephesus was known as the bank of Asia Minor. When Artemis's temple was destroyed in 365 B.C., Alexander the Great offered to rebuild it. The Ephesians turned down his proposal and built the temple with their own money, hiring the most famous artists of the time.

Not only was Ephesus a great place to live, it provided a strategic center for evangelistic work in that important part of the Roman world. Paul was warmly received by the Jewish community in Ephesus. He preached there for about three months, until they could not tolerate his message any longer. Paul then continued in a lecture hall next door to the synagogue. "This went on for two years," Luke reports, "so that all the Jews and Greeks who lived in the province of Asia heard the word of the Lord" (Acts 19:10). Paul also had a problem with the silversmiths, but that's another story (see Acts 19:24-41).

Mostly Ephesus was a cross-section of Roman and Greek culture, with its own version of the popular vices of the day. Recently, an economist with an international reputation said that if more than two percent of the people operating present-day financial institutions were dishonest, the system could not work. Since not much has changed across the centuries, it's fair to presume the same situation existed in ancient Ephesus. Most of the people were good citizens who tried to live honest, honorable lives.

But there were others.

In his first letter to Timothy, Paul listed some of the kinds of people who made up the darker, evil side of Ephesus (see 1:9-10). These also represented the unbelievers against which Christians were measured. Note the sort of people on Paul's list:

- *Lawbreakers:* These were not "accidental" sinners, people who didn't know God's law. The lawless deliberately sinned to satisfy their selfish desires.

- *Rebels:* People with no reverence for God.
- *The ungodly and sinful:* History's terrible twins, describing those who are deliberately unlike God.
- *The unholy and irreligious:* Could be translated "impious and polluted."
- *Those who kill their fathers and mothers:* Ancients considered this the worst of all sins. Under Roman law, these murderers were sewn into a bag that included a poisonous snake and then drowned.
- *Adulterers and perverts:* the leaders of sexual immorality.
- *Slave traders, liars, and perjurers.*

What a terrible list! They were the worst of the unbelievers in the Ephesus Paul and Timothy knew. Yet, it was against these sinners that Christians were compared when Paul wrote, "If anyone does not provide for his relatives, and especially for his immediate family, he has denied the faith and is worse than an unbeliever" (5:8).

The Challenge Christians Faced in Ephesus

Paul, at the end of his ministry, gave some special instructions to Timothy, who was just starting out as a pastor. The apostle's words were not suggestions, however. He said, "This *command* I entrust to you, Timothy, my son" (1:18 NASB, emphasis added). The word "command" is a military word carrying the sense of urgent obligation. It has the force, though not the harshness, of the drill sergeant who said to his troops, "When I say, 'Jump,' I want you to say, 'How high?' on the way up."

Timothy was charged to "fight the good fight, holding on to faith and a good conscience" (vv. 18-19). In Ephesians 6:10-17, Paul called the church to battle. There, he described the Christian armor in detail. Here, Timothy and the Christians with whom he lived were instructed to fight the battle against sin. Their weapons against evil were to be an unshakable confidence in the message of Jesus and an unwavering commitment to live a clean life. Or, put more simply, they were to believe correctly and act rightly.

Paul's word to the Ephesians and to Timothy seem to be in tension, but they are not. Paul advised the Ephesians that to live for Christ is to guard against the pollution of a sinful world by careless and costly connections with unbelievers. On the other hand, Timothy and his friends were to live in such a way that their conduct was never an excuse for an unbeliever to choose not to follow Jesus.

Let's take a brief tour through 1 Timothy and note the instructions Paul gave concerning the reason why believers were to live lives of "faith and good conscience."

"Some have rejected these and so have shipwrecked their faith" (1:20). Hymenaeus and Alexander are identified as tragic examples who have separated faith and good conscience to their ruin. In 2 Timothy 2:17, Hymenaeus is also mentioned as a man whose teaching is like gangrene. Faith and a good conscience must be kept together for spiritual growth.

"I also want women to dress modestly . . . appropriate for women who profess to worship God" (2:9-10). This verse has been twisted to say things far different than the apostle intended. These words are clearly connected with the call for believers "to lift up holy hands in prayer, without anger or disputing" (v. 8). Stated most simply, whether men or women are involved, faith and a good conscience must be kept together for proper worship.

A church leader "must also have a good reputation with outsiders," so as not to "fall into disgrace and into the devil's trap" (3:7). Christian leaders, pastors, and laypeople live in a world that watches them closely. Unbelievers may not accept the teachings of Christ but often know what they are and expect those who guide the Church to live like Him. The combination of faith and a good conscience must be built into the lives of those would be leaders in the Kingdom.

"If anyone does not provide for his relatives, and especially for his immediate family, he has denied the faith and is worse than an unbeliever" (5:8). Here again, we have the call for all believers to combine faith and good conscience in all they do.

In the New Testament, there are two dominant words used for families. The first is *patria*, from which the English word "patriarch" is derived. *Patria* refers specifically to biological descent. The second Greek word used for families is *oikos*. *Oikos* is more common in the New Testament and signifies the broader concept of household.

In Roman and Jewish first-century cultures, *oikos* referred to a social unit, consisting of all those dependent upon the head of a house. A household included everyone from biological sons and daughters to servants and in-laws. That concept of a household is more broad than contemporary notions of the nuclear family unit. In this setting, there was a strong awareness of interdependence and responsibility of household members to one another in times of need. The household was the primary source of assistance when difficulties arose.

Paul's words about family support cannot be separated from the discussion of widows in the Early Church, which precedes and follows it. Married women had the security of their husbands and the support of their families. The life of a widow, however, in the first-century world was more tragic than we might imagine in our day of multiple care systems. Young widows might, and in that culture probably should, marry again. Older widows had nothing. No inheritance. No social security. No welfare. Nothing. If the Church did not help, these widows were in deep trouble.

And the world was watching.

Conclusion

The apostle Paul had a significant influence on the formation of the Early Church. His journeys took him along the rim of the Mediterranean Sea from Israel to Rome. And everywhere he went, he established new churches. However, it was impossible for Paul to stay and be a resident pastor to all the churches he helped to start. He was able to return to some of the churches during subsequent missionary journeys. At other times, Paul kept in touch through written letters and messengers. Several of his letters are contained in the New Testament. In these letters, we gain a sense of Paul's intense interest to see these churches grow and mature in their faith.

In the Scripture passage we have examined in this chapter, Paul wrote to advise and encourage Timothy, the young pastor of the church at Ephesus, about several specific matters: the integrity of church leaders, the correction of false teachers, and the importance of sound doctrine.

Paul also addressed a problem that transcends cultural boundaries: How do we care for the most destitute people in the church? Paul's advice to Timothy regarding the care of widows reminds us that our faith in Christ calls us to care for the sick, the poor, and the marginalized.

Paul's words also included a saying that sounds harsh: "If anyone does not provide for his relatives, and especially for his immediate family, he has denied the faith and is worse than an unbeliever." Nevertheless, Paul was not engaging in overstatement to make a point. He meant what he said. In that day, if parents were in need, Greek law required that grown children must support them, and offenders were threatened with the loss of their civil rights. It was hard for Paul to imagine that pagans could exemplify Christ's love more effectively than believers could. For followers of Christ, this is more than a social obligation. It is an authentic expression of faith that is consistent with the example that Jesus has modeled for us.

Paul's message is clear. If a person's love for his or her neighbors does not begin at home, then the claim that he or she loves God is a lie. And liars are not better than any unbeliever.

May we live such authentic lives of faith in Christ that no such charge can ever be directed at any of us.